Albourne to Ditchling.

Along the Greensand Ridge

MARK DUDENEY AND EILEEN HALLETT
Illustrated by Mark Dudeney

Mid-Sussex Books

First published in 2000 by
Mid-Sussex Books
4 Crescent Road
Burgess Hill
West Sussex
RH15 8EG

ISBN 0 9530625 97

Printed in Great Britain by
Delta Press 2 Goldstone Street, Hove BN3 3RJ

Acknowledgements

We would like to express our gratitude to the Editor of the *Mid Sussex Times* and the Editor and Proprietor of the *Hassocks and Keymer Talkabout* for permission to quote from their respective publications.

Special thanks are also due to:

Mr Norman Whall and his sister, Ruby, for providing us with so many valuable sources of information.

Mr Ray Packham for his advice, interest and support.

Mr Roger Packham for so generously allowing us to illustrate the work with photographs from his private collection.

Mrs Mary Shelton for permitting us to quote from her wartime diaries and other memoirs.

Mr Terry Edgeler for granting us sight of official documents relating to his grandfather's police career.

Mr Brian Hudson for giving us access to the records of Vine Cottage.

Mr Charles Wyatt and Jim and Barbara Osborne.

Other contributors include:

The late Cyril Charman; the late George Cragg, Mrs Janet Cragg , Curator of Ditchling Museum; Mrs Peggy Dudeney; Mr John Fernee; Mrs Judy Fuller; Mrs Liz Middleton of the West Sussex County Council Library Services; Mrs Susan Muir, Mrs Mary Offer; Mr Nigel Orlebar; and Mrs Janet Slaughter.

We also wish to thank Rose Dudeney, editor, and Mark Leo Dudeney for their work on the manuscript.

Contents

Rooks: Spring-nesting in Danny Park

Introduction

Through the pages of this book, we journey east along the road that links Albourne with Ditchling. For most of the way it follows the high ground along the greensand ridge, which is a seam of soft sandstone that may occasionally be seen in the form of rocky outcrops.

Such conditions do not feature widely in the geology of Sussex, but nevertheless are of considerable importance, as they support the most fertile soil in the county, and those who farm it, enjoy distinct advantages over their neighbours stuck in Gault or Wealden clay. The Romans, who were here for nearly four hundred years, certainly appreciated its friable nature, and evidence of their occupation is still being discovered. However, apart from the odd reference or two, we will not be harking back to those distant times, but concentrating more on the people whose presence and contributions helped to make and shape Mid Sussex into the rural district it used to be.

No reference is made of the Chinese Gardens at Hurstpierpoint, or the Orchard Tea Gardens in Hassocks because space, or the lack of it, will not permit their inclusion. But we intend to make good the omission in a forthcoming book, which provisionally entitled *The Pleasure Gardens of Sussex*, will deal exclusively with the subject, and also include the history of such places as Swiss Cottage and the Devil's Dyke. Also, we have said nothing about Butting Hill or the land around Stone Pound, for that was dealt with in our previous publication *From Pyecombe to Cuckfield.*

Change is a continuing process. Our forefathers would hardly recognise the area as it is now. And equally, in years to come, people may well find it difficult to believe, that at one time, green fields, leafy woods and quiet places separated the communities in which they live. It is to them, and those who follow them, that these memories are dedicated.

"When time who steals our years away
Shall steal our pleasures too,
The memory of the past will stay
And half our joys renew".
"Then refill the bowl, away with gloom,
Our joys shall always last;
For hope will brighten days to come
And memory gild the past."

– Moore

Albourne

The King's Head ~ The Yellow Car Mystery ~ The London Road ~ Will Medhurst ~ James Starley ~ St. Bartholomew's Church ~ Albourne Place ~ Sidney Hole ~ The Onion Fields

In his book *Highways and Byways in Sussex*, Mr E. V. Lucas says

> Less than two miles west of Hurstpierpoint is Albourne, so hidden away that one might know this part of the country well and yet be continually overlooking it. The western high road between London and Brighton passes within a stone's throw of Albourne, but one never suspects the existence, close by, of this retired village, so compact and virginal and exquisitely old-fashioned.

These words were written nearly one hundred years ago and are as true now as they were then. Nowadays all that most people using the main road ever notice, is a rather conspicuous property facing the lane leading to Hurstpierpoint. Built in the 1930s, it was once a public house called the King's Head that had been constructed on the site of an earlier coaching inn bearing the same name. The former building had been a favourite meeting place for generations of villagers, but was ill-equipped to cater for the rapid increase in traffic, or to meet the demands imposed by the burgeoning charabanc trade. Therefore and despite local objections, it was knocked down. Gone for ever was the old-fashioned inn with its ivy-clad walls and flag-stone floor, and gone too were many of its patrons who felt alienated by the brash and dazzling edifice that had risen in their midst. Brash it undoubtedly was – dazzling too – for the dominant feature was a huge central dome entirely sheathed in copper, an embellishment that prompted a village wag to describe the building as:

> A sort of cross between a cinema, St. Paul's Cathedral and an observatory!

The metallic roof came into its own during the long summer evenings, when it was transformed by the rays of the setting sun into a glowing orb, or as someone unkindly observed, a "gigantic blood orange". It was certainly eye catching and swiftly became a well-known landmark, not only from the road, but also from the air, which was surely the architect's intention. He could not have foreseen however that in just a few short years, the crowning glory of his achievement would have to be camouflaged lest it serve as a navigational aid for enemy aircraft. But that is what happened, the shining sphere was coated in paint, and to the best of our knowledge, has remained so ever since.

The new King's Head – the small paddock on its southern side was known as the Platt. It was the regular site for the village fair. Messrs Harris provided the thrills and spills, and the occasion was also used to distribute the village social club's annual payout. During the Second World War, the beer cellar doubled up as an air-raid shelter, providing sanctuary for the landlord's family and local children.

The former King's Head public house at Albourne, with the landlord, Mr Ware, standing at the entrance

The Yellow Car Mystery

During 1908, when motor cars were a comparatively novel feature of the highway, an accident involving a couple of them occurred on the London Road near the King's Head. One, in the act of overtaking, collided with the other and caused it to crash. To make matters worse, the offending vehicle failed to stop. The matter was reported in the *Mid Sussex Times*:

> A party of London motorists met with a serious mishap at Albourne on Sunday evening. The car in which they were travelling was struck by a yellow car, the rear wheels went up in the air and the party was thrown out.

The Hurstpierpoint Policeman, PC Edgeler, together with various onlookers, examining the damaged vehicle after it had been towed from the scene of the accident and parked at the King's Head.

> Mr and Mrs Jones of High Road, Streatham, and their son were badly cut about the head and face, another son had a thigh fractured and was conveyed to hospital, while Mr Wilkie, also of London, had a severe gash in the leg. All were much bruised and suffered from shock. They were subsequently taken to Brighton. The police have not, so far, succeeded in tracing the yellow car. Sergeant Waghorn of Lewes left for London this Tuesday morning to continue investigations.

The incident, which quickly became known as the 'Yellow Car Mystery', attracted considerable newspaper attention, and in consequence, Sergeant Waghorn received several tips regarding the make of the vehicle and the identity of its owner. This eventually resolved in his interviewing a Mr John William Cecil Dones, and reporting that gentleman for driving a motor car on a certain highway at a speed which was dangerous to the public, having regard to all the circumstances. (Oddly, no mention was made of damage or injury.). The ensuing case, which was heard at Haywards Heath Magistrates Court, excited a lot of public interest, not for the least reason, that the accused – a wealthy and elegant young man about town – was also brother to the well-known and much photographed Edwardian actresses and society beauties, Zena and Phyllis Dare, young ladies whose smiling faces appeared regularly on theatre hoardings throughout the land.

On the date of the hearing, Dones drove down to Haywards Heath in his car, a Charron, which he parked in front of the court building. Mr Lawson Lewis appeared for the prosecution, and Mr E. E. Humphrys for the defence. In answer to the formal charge, the defendant entered a plea of 'Not guilty'.

When questioned as to his movements at the time and date in question, Dones readily admitted that he was driving north on the Brighton road with a male companion. However he flatly denied

Miss Phyllis Dare and her brother, Mr John William Cecil Dones
Miss Zena Dare

being either involved in, or aware of, an accident or altercation with any other vehicle. He had driven, he said, from Brighton to Crawley at a speed rarely reaching, and never exceeding, thirty miles an hour.

Witness for the prosecution, Mr Herbert Edward Cooper, stated that at the relevant time, he was cycling towards Brighton, when he saw two cars approaching abreast of each other. The one on the nearside was of a dark green colour, while that on the offside was pale primrose or pale lemon chrome. There were two men in this car, the vehicles drew close together and the green car mounted the grass verge. Then he heard a bang, after which the driver of the green vehicle appeared to lose his grip of the steering wheel and the control of the car. It turned a complete somersault, the occupants were thrown out while the other vehicle, with the driver fighting for control, zigzagged up the road towards him. As it passed, the witness shouted out but was ignored. Mr Cooper who noticed that the driver and his companion occupied bucket seats, estimated that the motor was travelling at approximately fifty miles an hour. He said that he had a clear view of the vehicle, he particularly noticed its bonnet which he described as torpedo-shaped. He had not seen one like it since, at least, not until arriving at court that day, when he saw it parked outside. He went on to positively identify it as the car that had driven off from the accident – and he identified Dones as the driver.

At first sight this appeared to be a pretty damning state of affairs, especially as Dones' car was a pale cream colour. But crucially for the defendant, it did not have bucket seats, and there was nothing to indicate that they had ever been fitted. More importantly, there was absolutely no sign of damage to the vehicle or any suggestion of recent repair work. But what clinched the Defence's case was the statement of an independent witness who had been driving south and came upon the scene of the accident. He said that upon reaching the foot of Handcross hill, a bright yellow racing car travelling in the opposite direction had nearly put him in the ditch!

In view of this sworn testimony, and Mr Cooper's inconsistency relating to the matter of bucket seats, the magistrates were left with little choice but to dismiss the case. But their unease at the decision was reflected in the instruction that each party should pay its own costs.

The London Road

A varied and colourful stream of characters have bypassed Albourne over the years, but surely none more so than those described by old James Nye on the occasion of his golden wedding in 1910. Reminiscing about his youth, he said:

I remember the old coaching days. They used to keep between eighty and a hundred horses down at Stroods. Mr Samuel Goodman lived there then, and he drove a coach himself. The coaches passed through Hickstead – about forty a day. Of the drivers, there was Bob Snow, a regular old whip, and Brackenbury, who drove 'The Morning Times'. Mr Goodman also drove that, and the best horses were on that coach. I can remember the postboys who used to be at Hickstead when Mr Johnson kept 'The Castle'. I can see some of them now, in white breeches, top boots, blue jackets and tall hats – each riding one horse and leading another. There were Jack Matthews, Peter Newnham, Charlie Papsworth and Lucas. These were 'first-turn' boys and never had any wages, but depended on tips for a living. And they lived well! The 'second-turn' boys had so much a week. There were some pretty narrow escapes through using a colt or two in the coaches, and once a coach rolled over in the ditch and shot all the passengers into a field!

In later years, in addition to the thousands of wayfarers who travelled the road in the normal course of business, there was an extrovert minority, the type of people who used the highway as a platform on which to demonstrate their own peculiar talents and abilities. An example of the sort of person we mean was the blind pedestrian who annually walked from Brighton to London unaccompanied. Then there was an Irishman who pushed a barrow-load of bricks from Hyde Park Corner to the Aquarium. He had a rival, a gentleman who performed a similar task, but carried his bricks in a hod. There was also a cyclist who passed through the district on a bicycle fitted with only one wheel. Of him, the *Mid Sussex Times* remarked:

> His performance was watched with great interest by many people who marvelled at the clever manner in which he negotiated the traffic.

Imagination has been stretched to the limit in devising different and crowd pleasing ways of making the trip. Contestants have walked the road backwards, they have pushed lawnmowers, and have been transported squeezed up in prams. On one occasion it was announced that a farmer from Natal intended to cover the distance on the back of an ostrich! But whether the event actually took place we have been unable to establish.

However, there surely has never been a more unusual method than that adopted by a pretty young Frenchwoman by the name Mademoiselle Florence. Known as the Lady Globe Walker, she made the journey on a ball weighing 71 pounds. She was allowed to dismount for a short time after passing each milestone, but otherwise

Mademoiselle Florence, the Lady Globe Walker

only three hours rest were permitted in every twenty-four. Despite such gruelling conditions, she eventually arrived at Brighton Aquarium at 2.45am on Sunday 21st June 1903, having taken a week to complete the task, during which time she had worn out seven pairs of boots.

Will Medhurst

To the south of the King's Head and on the same side of the road, a flint-walled terrace of single-storied dwellings huddles beneath the wayside bank. Known as Butts Cottages, they were former farm stables that had become surplus to requirements and so were converted into homes for farm workers. Many years later, evidence of their original use could still be seen in the form of large iron tethering rings that remained in the wall alongside the doorways. One of the tenants was Will Medhurst, a carter who worked at a nearby farm. he died in 1943, but is still remembered with great affection by many senior villagers, one of whom, Mrs Barbara Osborne, née Goldsmith, had this to say:

> Mr Medhurst had two mares, Violet and Blossom. He thought the world of those horses and it was a real pleasure to watch him handling them. Violet was a bit on the frisky side, whereas Blossom was as gentle and docile as could be. I will never forget how at the end of the day, he would lead them from the stable at Barleycroft, down the street, and then on to Yew Tree House where they grazed in the cricket field overnight. I made sure he saw me, because I knew I would be lifted onto Blossom's back and taken for a ride down the lane.

Mr Charles Wyatt who left Hurstpierpoint school at the age of fourteen, and went to work at the wheelwright's yard next to the smithy at Albourne Green, recalled an occasion when one of Will Medhurst's mares went lame with a suspected abscess in the frog of its hoof:

Will Medhurst

The Smithy, Albourne

> The blacksmith removed the shoe, cut into the hoof and exposed the abscess. He then applied a linseed poultice which he wrapped in sacking and bound round the affected area. Sounds simple enough, but in fact it was a long and difficult operation, at the end of which the horse was fairly distressed. Will (Mr Medhurst), remained with her in the forge all night. He didn't leave until later the following day, and then only when he felt quite certain that she would recover.

Charles Wyatt also recalled that Will was a champion ploughman. "There were sixteen ferrules on his whip," he said. "Each one represented a major trophy that he had won."

When Will Medhurst died, his coffin was placed on a Sussex farm wagon, which drawn by his old horses, Violet and Blossom, was conveyed to Albourne churchyard where he was laid to rest close to the fields where he worked all his life. A simple gravestone marks the spot, but the inscription thereon reveals nothing of the character or history of the man, so, in some small part at least, we hope to have preserved his memory.

James Starley

Beyond Butts Cottages, and on the eastern side of the highway – which is the parish boundary with Hurstpierpoint – stands Woodbine Cottage, the childhood home of one of Albourne's most famous sons, the inventor, James Starley, a person often referred to as 'the father of the cycle industry'.

According to Mr H. W. Barfleet in an article that was written for the *Irish Cyclist* magazine on the 19th May 1920:

> Of the name and personalities which have helped to compile cycle history, none stand out so prominently as that of James Starley. He was born on the 21st April 1830, in an old cottage, [The Arches, Albourne Street] which I believe still stands about a hundred yards from London Road. Here he lived until he was four years old, when his father moved to Woodbine Cottage, opposite the London Road. He went to school at Spring Cottage [He was taught by a Miss Osborn], where history records that he was considered to be a dull boy. After two and a half years there, he left and went to the National School at Hurstpierpoint, where he remained until 1841, when he started work on his father's farm [Later known as Hazelden's nursery]. He was more at home there, as he could handle a plough and soon showed those marvellous powers of observation which were later to be so useful to him.

Woodbine Cottage – this building was demolished and then rebuilt to the east when the A23 was widened.

> As an instance, he noticed that rats had made a regular pathway behind the pigstyes, and having no trap, he told his brother John that he would contrive something to catch the rodents, which he did, in a primitive form. Taking the steel rib of an old umbrella, he ground one end to a sharp point and secured it to the branch of a willow tree by a piece of string, placing a lever so that when a rat trod on it, the skewer was released. John ridiculed the idea, saying that he would eat any rats which were caught. The first morning after the trap was set, James got up early to see the results of his experiment, and soon returned to John's bedside with a rat on the skewer, saying "Here's your breakfast, John." With this, his earliest invention, he rid the place of vermin.

Starley worked on his parents' farm until 1846, during which year he had a difference of opinion with his father, so divisive, that he sought his fortune elsewhere. In the words of Mr Barfleet:

> He returned home, packed his scanty belongings into a handkerchief, and without even saying goodbye, started like many another, for London, that goal which the rustic mind then – as now – pictures as paved with gold. He stayed one day at Little Horsted, where his brother William was gardener to Sir Humphrey Moon, and then proceeded on through Tunbridge Wells and Tonbridge to the bottom of River Hill, where he earned a shilling for helping to push a heavily-laden cart up the hill. He arrived at Lewisham footsore and hungry, and with only a few pence in his pocket. Next morning he obtained work on the farm of a Mr Wyatt, a strawberry grower. At the end of his day's work, Starley was seen by his employer to be walking lame, his feet being tender after his long tramp. Saying "We want no cripples here", the boss told the foreman to pay him off, and he was given two shillings and threepence.

Not deterred by such harsh treatment, Starley remained in Lewisham, first obtaining lodgings, and then a job as undergardener at John Penn's, the engineers, where, as Mr Barfleet says:

> Part of his duty was to wheel his employer to the works in a bathchair, and while waiting for him Starley had access to the works and obtained his first knowledge of engineering methods. About this time, he took to cleaning the watches of the workmen, and although a big man with large hands, he could handle the delicate mechanism of a watch with wonderful nicety.

It was during his employment at Penn's that Starley's genius began to flower. He invented a number of things including a cleverly designed window blind and an adjustable candlestick, while in his leisure time he repaired pianos, knife cleaning machines and clocks. He left Penn's in 1859 and went to Newton, Wilson and Company of Holborn, London, who were sewing machine manufacturers. While employed by them he improved their machines and mastered the mechanism to such an extent, that in 1861, he produced a machine designed to stitch round the edges of cuffs or the bottom of trouser legs after they were made up (later known as the European sewing machine). This machine was made during his spare time in a small room at his home where he had constructed a crude lathe.

Seeing the potential of the invention, Starley, together with a fellow employee, Mr Josiah Turner, and an American named Salisbury, left Newton, Wilson and Co., and went to Coventry to embark in the sewing machine trade. They did not succeed. However, the new business attracted attention, and a number of gentlemen of position who had the welfare of their fellow citizens at heart, formed a company, and the services of Turner and Starley were retained. The business prospered and the products manufactured under Starley's superintendence included the 'European', 'Godiva', 'Express' and

'Swiftsure' sewing machines, all of which were invented and patented by him.

During this period, Starley had become interested in improving the design and performance of cycles, with the result that around 1865, he produced a four wheeled velocipede with suspension wheels. He became more and more involved in this sort of work and eventually went into business on his own account. To list his achievements in the years that followed would be a prodigious task. It is sufficient to say his greatest invention was the differential gear and a tricycle christened 'the Salvo', the first machine to be fitted with the device. As Mr Barfleet says:

> Orders came rolling in. Agents were appointed all over the country, and it was in 1880 when a Miss Roach, daughter of the Newport, Isle of Wight agent, was riding a Salvo, that the tricycle came under the notice of Queen Victoria, who commanded the young lady's presence at Osborne House, with the result that Her Majesty ordered two tricycles. They were despatched in January, 1881, Starley accompanying them to Osborne.

At the time of delivery, Starley's days were numbered, and he was aware of it, having previously discovered a lump on his right side, which he had correctly diagnosed as cancer. He died six months later on the 17th June, 1881, leaving a widow, Jane, four sons and two daughters.

Thus passed a man who gave his ideas freely to his fellows, for he never made a fortune from his inventions. However, this Albourne farmer's son will not be forgotten by the world he benefited, and certainly not in Coventry, where a fine monument to his memory, subscribed for by the citizens, was unveiled on the 8th of November 1884.

St. Bartholomew's Church

On the other side of the road to Woodbine Cottage, a narrow lane winds its way through the fields and ends abruptly at St. Bartholomew's, which is surely one of the prettiest churches in Sussex. Nestling so naturally in the surrounding countryside, its weathered stone and simplicity of design gives an air of antiquity. But appearances deceive, for while a place of worship has stood on the site for at least seven hundred years, the present building dates only from Victorian times.

Some parts of the older church remain, but because of earlier neglect, it was virtually rebuilt during a programme of restoration that commenced in 1853. This resulted in the transept being pulled down and a new north aisle being added to the nave.The original Norman arch of the chancel was replaced with a copy, while the carved stonework from the former was incorporated in the new churchyard wall. Happily, many historical features were retained, including some Jacobean woodwork in the chancel, and a memorial dated 1603 in the nave floor.

William Hill of London is credited with making the church organ in 1870. It was not commissioned for St. Bartholomew's , but rather a private residence at Witley, Surrey, where it remained until it was moved to St. Peter's Church at Hambledon (also in Surrey) in 1934. A further fifty-seven years were to elapse before it arrived – rather worse for wear – at Albourne in 1991, and since then, no effort has been spared to restore the instrument to its former glory. According to the legend inscribed on a brass plaque within the church, timber used for the organ's renovation came from an oak tree that was blown down at Danworth Farm, Hurstpierpoint during the great gale of 1987. The bell turret originally contained two bells, now there is only one, but no matter, for according to the *Village Guide*:

> This bell constitutes one of the treasures of Albourne, it was made by Peter the Potter at some time between 1282 and 1307 and is thus one of the earliest bells to be found in Sussex. It is inscribed in Lombardic capitals, with a dedication to the Mother of God.

The original church at Albourne from a print by R. H. Nibbs

The present church

Albourne Place

Glancing from church to lane, it will be noticed that a large gatepost forms part of the fence bordering the field on the opposite side. It is all that remains of the entrance to a driveway (now ploughed up) that led to Albourne Place, the manor house of the village. Concealed from view, this property may be found halfway between St. Bartholomew's and Trusslers Hill Lane, and at one time was linked to both, thereby providing an appreciated short-cut for those who lived at the western boundary of the rural district. Successive residents at the big house had always permitted such use, and in the traditional manner of English squirearchy, closely involved themselves in local affairs. One occupant in particular, the later Sir Eric Geddes, a former chairman of British Airways was a great benefactor to the community, and he and Lady Geddes held splendid Christmas parties every year for the children of the village (an event that was carried on by the next resident – Mrs Crowther). It is perhaps also of interest to note that Sir Eric achieved a near unique position during the First World War, in that he held the rank of a General in the Army and an Admiral in the Navy at one and the same time.

Tommy Dudeney at the gatepost

Albourne Place dates from the 17th century, although interior examination suggests that a much earlier property has been incorporated into the present building. From a historian's point of view, it is probably best associated with an incident that is alleged to have occurred shortly after the end of the English Civil War. The mansion was then owned by a John Juxon, the person responsible for converting the premises to its existing semi-classical style. He had a brother named William, who was a churchman with powerful connections. Not only was Archbishop Laud his close friend and mentor, but the reigning monarch, Charles 1, also held him in high esteem. Benefiting from the association, William Juxon swiftly climbed the clerical tree, and in no time at all became the Bishop of London, and eventually, the Lord High Treasurer of England. But his elevation proved to be short-lived, for at the famous (or infamous) meeting of the Long Parliament in 1640, decisions were made concerning 'divine rights' that were to precipitate national conflict and bring about the downfall of the King. Anticipating the troubles ahead, Juxon resigned from his civil appointment. However, he was no 'fair weather friend', and remained devoted to Charles, even to accompanying him to the scaffold, an event that is touchingly described in an extract taken from *A History of the Castles, Mansions and Manors of Western Sussex*, first published in 1879.

Juxon, who was at the time, Bishop of London and Clerk of the Closet, received his Sovereign's last confidences. Turning to Dr Juxon, the King said – "I have a good cause and a gracious God is on my side."

Dr Juxon – "There is but one stage more, this stage is turbulent and troublesome. It is a short one; but you may consider it will soon carry you a very great way. It will carry you from earth to heaven, and there you will find a great deal of cordial joy and comfort."

The King – "I go from a corruptible to an incorruptible crown, where no disturbance can be; no disturbance in the world."

Dr Juxon – "You are exchanged from a temporal to an eternal

crown: a good exchange."

Then the King, taking off his cloak and his George, gave his George to Dr Juxon, saying: "Remember!"

For refusing to disclose this last conversation to the authorities, Juxon was himself committed to prison, and upon his release, retired to live with his brother and his family at Albourne Place – which brings us to the earlier mentioned incident.

It is said that Cromwell's men, still smarting from Juxon's resolve not to acquaint them with the King's last words, decided that he should be re-arrested and further questioned. Accordingly, a parliamentary force was despatched to Sussex with orders to bring him back, but on receiving warning of their approach, he disguised himself as a workman, ascended a ladder, and pretended to be engaged in the task of repairing a chimney stack. It was a brazen but successful subterfuge. After a long and fruitless search (all of which time he was in full view) his would-be captors rode off empty-handed.

That is the story – and perhaps it is true, the chances are, however, that it has been somewhat garnished by re-telling. What cannot be disputed is that many years later, long after all the actors of the drama had passed on, an intriguing discovery was made at Albourne Place. A mysterious chamber, the existence of which was previously unknown, and to which access could only be gained through a chimney, was uncovered by workmen constructing a passage between two rooms. Obviously intended as a secret compartment, it is tempting to believe that it was a refuge specially created to shelter Juxon at times of emergency. Should that have been the case, it is just possible that he was working on it when the officials unexpectedly arrived, in which event he would have had little choice but to carry on and hope for the best All this of course is pure speculation, the important thing is that he successfully evaded capture, and years later at the restoration, was rewarded with the Archbishopric of Canterbury, an office he held until his death in 1663.

Albourne Place

Sidney Hole

For centuries, farming and agriculture have been the premier industry of the district, as well as the greatest employer of labour, but not any more. Ploughmen, carters, herdsmen, together with associated village craftsmen such as the wheelwright, thatcher and blacksmith have long since vanished from the scene. But the land remains, and while walking round the silent fields it is not difficult to imagine how they must have been in former days. Farm workers then might have received little schooling, but were indisputedly wise in the ways of their world. The art of hedge-laying, or thatching a hayrick held no mysteries for them.

They knew the times to reap and sow, the land was their book, and its cultivation and upkeep, together with the welfare of the livestock it supported, was the foundation on which they developed their skills.

Will Goldsmith (on the left) and workmate, broadcasting corn at Inholmes Farm

Their employers, the farmers, also knew a thing or two, and Mid Sussex contained many such men. Outstanding amongst these were the Broads, both father and son who farmed at the Ham near Stone Pound. Then there was Edwin Street at Burgess Hill, Charles Tulley at Pangdean, Mr Robinson at Saddlescombe and later John Holman of Ditchling. But first and foremost was Sidney Hole, the well known and widely respected farmer, businessman and inventor from Albourne. About him the *Village Guide* ventures the following information:

> When he died in 1956, in his 89th year, he held a total of 70 patents, the best known of which was his coding machine which had attracted such interest at the London Business Efficiency Exhibition. He invented a spill-proof, thief-proof and dirt-proof milk churn which won first prize at the Dairy Show. He was also the patentee and maker of the well-known Manulectric milk trolley.

Farming was Sidney Hole's main interest in life, and for 60 years he lived and worked at Yew Tree Farm. In addition, he had farms at Brighton, Withdean, Patcham, Rottingdean, Hurstpierpoint, Lewes and Rodmell. He was the best known farmer in the south of England and on four consecutive occasions won first prize for the best managed and cultivated dairy farm. He later went into the milk trade, opening his first shop in Hove, and after building up a chain

Sidney Hole's famous Manulectric milk trolley

of such businesses, amalgamated with Davigdor Dairies, retaining the position of Chairman for many years.

Still remembered in Albourne circles, Sidney Hole was described as being a hard but fair master who at all times expected one hundred percent effort from his employees. A firm believer in the old adage, 'the farmer's foot is the best manure', he was here, there and everywhere, checking that the workforce was always fully engaged. He even went so far as to build a platform on the elevator and stood on this when the men were haymaking – to make sure it was being

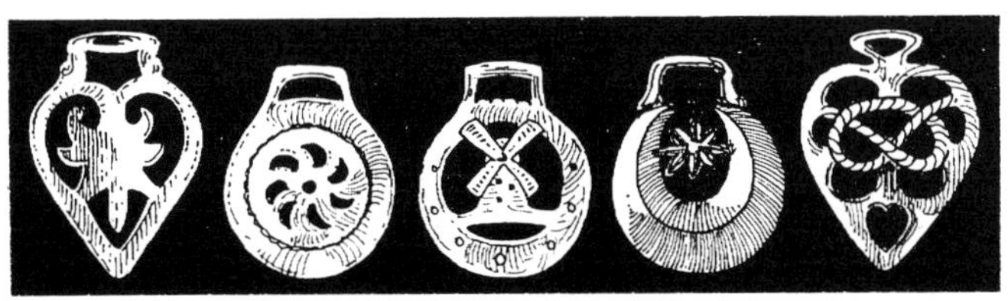

used to its full capacity! The story is told that on one occasion he came across a boy picking potatoes in a field, and because it was bitterly cold, the youngster had a hand tucked in his pocket, which caused the farmer to exclaim: "Now my lad, I work with both my hands, and where am I today?" To which the boy innocently replied: "Why, you be in the same field I be!"

Sidney Hole (left), George Goldsmith, and steam-hauled mole plough

The Street, showing 'Finches' on the left, and Curtain Cottage on the right. The W. I. Hall, a former First World War army hut, is on the centre/right of the picture.

The Onion Fields

As a result of the U-boat blockade in the north Atlantic during the early stages of the Second World War, self-sufficiency became a matter of the utmost importance to the people of this island, and all available land was cultivated in a national drive to increase the production of food. Sidney Hole's farms and market-gardens were no exception, and his sons George and Gilbert, who by then had taken over the day to day running of the business, were required to concentrate mainly on growing crops for seed.

With this in mind, acres of land were planted with a wide variety of vegetables, which included leeks, onions, carrots, potatoes, runner beans and sunflowers, as well as tomatoes, lettuce and cucumber. The last three were also grown for marketing. It was a labour intensive operation at a time when labour was in short supply, for the simple reason that most men of eligible age had been conscripted into His Majesty's forces. However, all was not lost, for just as they had in the 1914/18 conflict, the ladies came to the rescue, this time in the form of the Women's Land Army. In 1940, five or six such girls were employed at Albourne, one of whom was Mary Chesson, and within the space of a year she was to see the number of her colleagues increase to nearly one hundred! Some like Mary, lodged locally, while others were transported daily to and from towns on the south coast, but they were still too few to deal with the work, especially at harvest time. Then lorries would be driven down to Brighton on early closing day to pick up all the casual labour they could find. Even the lads from Hurstpierpoint College were permitted to neglect their studies in order to lend a hand. Mary, who kept a diary throughout the hostilities, was to refer to these and other matters in later years when she wrote a series of articles, collectively entitled *Life in the Land Army* which appeared in the now defunct *County Weekly Magazine*. The following extracts deal with the growing of onions. Sub-titled, 'Enough to make you cry' they provide a fascinating account of life on the land during that turbulent period.

Working on a market garden during the war, there was one vegetable with which we were involved every month of the year. This was the humble onion, although during the early forties it was not so humble, but a much sought-after prize. With imports almost non-existent, the British growers strived hard to fill the gap. We grew autumn-sown onions for pulling green in the spring, spring-sown onions for culinary use which were harvested late in the summer and then eventually, onions for seed.

Onions for spring pulling were usually sown about the middle of August They were the 'White Lisbon' type and were very hardy, never succumbing to the bad winter weather. They were sown with a hand drill as comparatively small amounts were grown, a half acre supplying a large number of spring onions. They germinated well in the warm soil and we would be push hoeing and hand hoeing them throughout September and October. Then, as soon as the soil was dry enough in the spring, say mid-February, we would be in there again. By the end of March they were large enough to pull and we would start getting orders from the wholesalers.

In the meantime, the soil was being prepared for the main crop onions. They were sown by large seed drills capable of sowing several rows at a time, and the appliances were drawn by either horse or tractor. Forty or fifty acres were grown by 1943, covering several fields. By the end of March the 'Big Hoe" commenced, the men push hoeing and the girls scratch hoeing. At the same time however, a considerable proportion of the workforce was involved in getting up market orders and keeping other crops under control. So as many casual staff as possible were brought in to help. People came from all quarters, many arriving daily from Brighton on the buses or in our farm lorries which picked them up at several points in the town.

I recall one group in particular, they had come for a week's working holiday. After starting hoeing, it was noticed that a member of their party, a woman, was moving very slowly and being left behind. The foreman thought he had better go and see what was holding her up. he came back looking very subdued. "Do you know what?" he said. "That lady is almost blind, she's weeding by touch, feeling which are onions and which are weeds – says she doesn't mind if we don't pay her the full wage, she wants to do her bit for the war effort, so who am I to stop her?" Despite her disability, the lady stayed the full week and for once the foreman went up in our estimation.

Onion bulbs that were grown for seed had been saved from the previous year's main crop, and at about the middle of February, we would begin to prepare for the planting. The fields chosen had already been cultivated in the autumn so that they were clean and free from weeds. Now they were to be ploughed again with horses, a single furrow at a time, and planted with onion bulbs about nine inches apart. Like everything else, the beds were hoed continuously throughout the summer, and in August the fields resembled a sea of large mauve coloured tennis balls, an absolute Mecca for bees. After a couple of weeks, the seed heads turned a dirty browney-grey and by the middle of September they were ready to be cut.

All the available labour was concentrated on this job. We worked in pairs, one girl holding the sack, the other cutting off the heads and stuffing them in. We swept through the fields like a swarm of locusts, leaving only the brown dry stalks in our wake. The drying equipment was unable to cope with the vast amount we collected so every evening while the picking was still in progress, lorries loaded high with sacks set off on the long journey to the Sussex/Kent border. The reason being that as the 'hop' harvest was already completed, ample facilities were available to dry the seed there. When this had been done, the flower heads were brought home again for threshing.

Collecting onion seed

> This was one of the dirtiest jobs going, and a miniature version of a corn thresher was used for the purpose. The waste was ground to dust and, as we worked inside a barn, there was nowhere for it to go, apart from over the workers. We wore masks but were sometimes almost choked by the browney-black powder. It was impossible to see from one side of the building to the other, and with the noise as well, most conversation was reduced to sign language. We covered ourselves with sacks, but the dust penetrated everything and at the end of the day, we looked like chimney sweeps.

Sometimes the war came uncomfortably close to home, and Mary describes two such occasions. The first occurred in the summer of 1942, when she recorded that a German aircraft dropped a string of bombs across the farm. One fell into a field of onions that was nearly ready for harvest:

> Next morning the local people strolled out to see the damage, especially souvenir-hunting youngsters on the look out for a piece of shrapnel. Our boss also did the rounds, and upon arriving at the field in question, nearly had a fit! People were not only trampling over his crops to gawp at the crater, but were helping themselves to onions in the process. Pockets were bulging and men were using their caps as baskets. The reek of burnt onions lingered in the air for days on end. Indeed, it was so strong that for the best part of the following week it could even be detected in Hurstpierpoint.

The second incident happened nearly two years later in February 1944. About fifty Land Army girls were picking out parsnips in the mill field, when it came on to rain so heavily that the foreman decided to call a halt:

> The carter and I unhitched the horses and set off back to the stable. We had just finished unharnessing them when we heard a plane coming down very low from the north. "One of ours looking for Jerries I expect," said the carter. He had hardly finished speaking when three loud thuds shook the ground. "By God! it is a b–Jerry!" he cried and we dashed to the stable door to see this great plane drop out of the cloud. It was so close we could see the pilot's face. The machine gun rattled, and then it was gone. When we went home, the carter's wife said that the road from the village had also been machine gunned as she was coming back on her bike. Luckily she wasn't hurt, but unfortunately people had been killed in the village, I think it was two or three adults and a child.

In the incident to which Mary refers, Heather Lamb, aged four, became Hurstpierpoint's one civilian casualty during the war. The German raider, a Dornier, first machine gunned the village, fracturing the gasometer in Western Road, then dropped its bombs. The little girl, who had been playing in her parents' garden at the time was killed by flying shrapnel. She is buried in the local cemetery and inscribed on her memorial stone are the words, "Killed by enemy action".

Land Army girls – setting off to work

Hurstpierpoint

Pesketts Mill ~ The Wood family ~ Pakyn's Manor~ Church of St. Lawrence ~ Church of Holy Trinity ~ Birds in Churches ~ The Reverend Cary Hampton Borrer ~ Entente Cordiale!~ School Days ~ PC Edgeler ~ The Road to Uganda ~ Thomas Marchant ~ Danny House and the Campions

Running straight as an arrow, the road from Albourne to Hurstpierpoint bridges a cutting through which a constant stream of traffic flows along the modern highway to Brighton. How different it would have appeared many years ago. A glance to the south then, and the only observable movement apart from the wheeling rooks and grazing cattle, would have been the revolving sweeps of an old post-mill that stood nearby.

In her book, *Memories of Hurst,* Vivienne Manchester states that the mill belonged to Pakyn's Manor, and stood in a copse! This seems an extraordinary choice for a site. Martin Brunnarius in his definitive study, *Windmills of Sussex*, says that it was known as Peskett's Mill, and this has been confirmed by local people to whom we have spoken. In all probability it was connected with a Hurstpierpoint corn merchant of the same name. Sadly it was either pulled down, or fell down in the late nineteenth century, and now nothing remains to mark its precise position. But we know that the mill was still operating in 1853, because a former resident of the village, Mr William Wood, says as much in his book, *A Sussex Farmer.* It was worked by his father, but frustratingly, apart from one brief mention, Mr Wood fails to provide any further information as to the place or its history.

The Wood Family

Before continuing on our way, it would be remiss of us not to provide the reader with more information concerning the Wood family, which is worth recording. Mr Wood Senior lived a long life to the full, and during its course, is said to have "contributed great benefit to friend and stranger alike". A native of Hurstpierpoint, he resided at a house called The Knolls, and in 1856, took office as the parish constable. He was eventually to become the assessor and collector of taxes, the parish road surveyor, and the churchwarden. That was not all, for he was elected as the Chairman of the Burgess Hill Water Company, and also as Chairman of the Burgess Hill Gas Company. In addition he acted as Chairman of the Hurstpierpoint Parish Council, and was a diligent member of the Cuckfield Board of Guardians and Rural District Council. At the same time, this tireless man operated three mills, had a large business in Brighton, and also farmed on an extensive scale, having no fewer than 1200 acres to his name. How he managed to attend to his public duties and private business so well, was best known to himself.

But life was not all work. At a hunt breakfast, no one could make a merrier speech or tell a humorous story half as effectively as Mr Wood and wherever he went, he was always a welcome guest. He retired in 1908 at the age of eighty-two, and then his son, the author, another genial and talented man, took control of the family business. He (the son) was the last person to operate the Clayton windmills as a going concern, and in due course, wrote most interestingly about them and other mid Sussex matters in the autobiography to which we have referred.

West Town

The Chairman and Board of the Burgess Hill Water Company outside the Pumping Station at Clayton

Pakyn's Manor

Having paid our respects to the Wood family, we enter the western extremity of the village of Hurstpierpoint, an area that was once widely known as West Town. Here, on the southern side of the road, and concealed behind a wall of flint and stone, stands a truly ancient and picturesque L-shaped building known as Pakyn's Manor. The name has been variously spelt over the years, as 'Paken's' and also 'Pacons'. (This last was found carved upon a pew in the old parish church of St. Lawrence). At one time the property was only second in social status to Danny, and much of its history may be found in volume XI of the *Sussex Archaeological Collections*. There we learn that its name derives from a gentleman called Paganus, who in 1157 was the Sheriff of Sussex. He was thought to have been connected with the Pierpoints, who were the early possessors of the Manor of Hurst (as the village was originally called). It would appear that the name Paganus changed to Pakyn fairly swiftly and certainly before 1216, for on that date it is recorded that Walter Pakyn lived at the manor. His descendants continued to reside there for nearly 300 years. The last to bear the name at that address was Roger Pakyn in 1509.

Thereafter many different families have resided at the property. There were the Burtenshaw's (one of whom is reputed to have committed murder). They were followed by Richard Holden, and through him, the Luxfords and the Fynes (or Fiennes). After which came the Threels, the Shorts, the Scrases and the Whitpaines. Thomas Butcher was next, and he brings us to the 18th century and to the Borrers, whose descendants remained in residence up to the 1930s. To the confusion of historians and researchers alike, five generations of this family baptised their sons William, so for the sake of simplicity, we will refer to them numerically.

William (1) the first Borrer to occupy Pakyn's, came from Bishophurst, the now extinct manor in Albourne. His son, William (2) was the High Sheriff for the county, and he it was who raised the 'Troop of Horse' for defence against Napoleon. As a result, and for

Archway in garden of Pakyn's Manor, which was constructed with masonry from the demolished parish church of St Lawrence

many years after, a field to the south of the property which had been used by the soldiery, was known as "Camp Platt". The next William (3), was a distinguished botanist, and the garden at the Manor owed much to his skilful planting. He then went to live at Barrow Hill, Henfield, having let Pakyn's for forty years to his younger brother Nathaniel (father of the Rev. Cary Hampton Borrer). William (3)'s son, William (4) resided at Cowfold. He was a respected ornithologist and author and his book, *The Birds of Sussex*, is keenly sought by collectors. His son, William (5) returned to Pakyn's when the forty-year lease expired. He died in 1920 and his daughter and son-in-law, Dr and Mrs Orlebar, followed in turn by their son, Nigel, remained in residence until the decision was reached to end the family occupancy and split the Manor into separate privately owned apartments or flats, and that is how it remains to this day.

Pakyn's Manor

Church of St. Lawrence

The original church at Hurstpierpoint was dedicated to St. Lawrence, a minor Spanish saint who was renowned for his zeal with regards to the care and protection of old folk. There is some dispute about its origins. There are those who believe that it was built by Simon de Pierpoint in the reign of Edward III, while others suggest that the person responsible for its construction was a certain John Urry, who was the village rector between 1419 and 1440. The following description of the place is contained in a rare 1875 publication entitled *Nooks and Corners of old Sussex* by the Reverend P. de Putron M.A., a former Rector of Rodmell:

> The existing edifice consists of a nave with gallery at the west end. a south aisle and gallery, a small north transept and two chancels – that which ranges with the south aisle is called the Danny chancel. At the west end is a substantial tower, containing six bells, a clock

Church of St. Lawrence from an engraving by S. C. Utting

> and a set of chimes, above which rises a wooden shingled spire of considerable height. The roof is curiously ornamented with various devices, carved in wood, of lions, eagles, fleurs -de-lis, keys, arrow-heads, portcullises, true-lovers knots, crowns, circular arches, compasses, cinquefoils and the arms of the Pierpoint family. Under an arch in the Danny chancel is the effigy of a Knight Templar, in chain armour, with his long and taper sword on his left side, his plain shield placed over his left shoulder. In the same chancel was an effigy in stone of a warrior, represented in plated armour of the fourteenth century, his head resting on his helmet, visor lifted up, at his feet as dog.

In fact the old church had been woefully neglected and by 1841, was in real danger of falling down. The same year heralded the arrival of a new Rector. Cary Hampton Borrer, M.A., late of Oriel College, Oxford, and the only son of the previously mentioned Nathaniel Borrer of Pakyn's Manor. He, according to William Wood, was:

> ...a young man, only just over twenty-one, full of zeal for the new movement towards reform in the services of the Church. He was faced with obstacles at every turn. The people were ready to grumble at any sign of High Church practices; the church wardens obstinate and jealous, objecting to change of any sort or kind. The church, a very old one, and chiefly built of timber, was in a ruinous condition, the interior dark and badly kept, a heavy gallery, high box pews, no choir or musical arrangements beyond a bass viol and two or three violins, and as I say, a determination on all sides that what had been good enough for their fathers and grandfathers was good enough for them.

However, it soon transpired that the Rector not only had a will and determination as strong as his parishioners, but also possessed a diplomacy and good nature that nothing could disturb. In the words of Mr Wood:

> I knew him closely for many years, part of the latter years of his ministry as churchwarden, yet I never saw him lose his temper, or his cheerful manner, however fierce and trying the opposition might prove to be; and in his early days he was constantly called to preside at meetings where he alone preserved a calm demeanour, his opponents meanwhile in a state bordering on fury.

In view of its inadequacy, the Reverend Borrer was determined that the old village church should be demolished, so that a new and more elegant building might rise in its place. An indication of his resolve is contained in a vestry book record of the very first meeting he presided over, which was held at the New Inn on October 22, 1841. The initial resolution reads:

> Measures should be adopted for rebuilding or enlarging the Parish Church, and that a committee be appointed to ascertain the various modes of raising money for its enlarging or rebuilding, and report their opinions at a future meeting.

The cause for this discussion had arisen as a result of an earlier receipt of letters from the Rural Dean and Archdeacon. In them they expressed complete agreement with the ambitious plans of the Reverend Borrer, adding rather astonishingly, that the original building housed nothing warranting preservation!

Such powerful support must have pleased the Rector, but the contention that there was nothing worthy of preservation was controversial to say the least. We have already mentioned the Knight Templar and the Warrior in the Danny chancel. In addition there was a Saxon font, and it is a sad reflection of the lack of interest in archaeology at the time, that neither the Dean, nor the Archdeacon, nor the Rector himself, made any illusion at all to these ancient relics. Thankfully the effigies were saved when the church was eventually pulled down. So was the door and piscina[1], the first going to Poynings church, and the second to Albourne. But the 800 year old font vanished into thin air! That it was eventually traced and recovered was entirely due to the unflagging efforts of Mr John Edwin Couchman, a keen antiquarian who, thirty years later, had come to live at Hurstpierpoint where he had a brewery. "He," says Mr Wood:

> ...knew of the Saxon font, described as one of the treasures of the old church, was greatly disturbed to find that it had disappeared and promptly began a search for it. From an old man who worked on Little Park Farm in the late churchwarden's time (who was then the occupier) he learnt that the font was brought to the farm with other stone and timber, was placed against the wall of one of the pigsties, and turned upside down. It formed a convenient stepping-stone when feeding the pigs. But it was gone again. Where was it now? The old man was able to tell him that one day the owner of the farm, the landlord, came along, was attracted by this peculiar appendage of the pigsty and stopped to examine it. He then decided that whatever it was (he did not know) it deserved a better place than this, told his tenant so, asked him what it really was, and when he was told, had it removed and taken to his house, to his conservatory, where it was ultimately found by Mr Couchman promoted to forming a flower pot for geraniums. It was an easy matter to persuade the old gentleman that its proper place was the parish church, to which it was restored, and again put to its original use.

As may be imagined, the proposals to pull down the old church and build a new one were strenuously opposed at first, but at last it was decided that it should be done. The estimated cost was between £5500 and £6000, £3000 of which was provided by large subscriptions, principally from the Campion and Borrer families (the latter also provided the stone of which the church was built) and a further considerable sum of money, came from Diocesan funds. Then the work commenced. The old ruin was pulled down, and the present building was erected in its place, the architect being Sir James Barry, who also designed St. Peter's Church at Brighton, and the Houses of Parliament. At this point one might have reasonably supposed that all the doubters had been won over – but none of it, the Rector still met opposition to all his minor requests for improved services, as Mr Wood relates:

> He wanted a new organ, better choir service, better light for the evening service, more frequent and earlier communion services, and white surplices. He also wanted an extension to the church yard, with a decent fence or wall around it, instead of the ruined fence then existing: and his vestrymen did not want any of these things, no change at all for them. The records of the old vestry book provide evidence enough of this. They disallowed the candles for evening service – later they voted for them. The meeting called to consider the enlargement of the churchyard, and fencing it, was 'dissolved' , they would not even discuss it, but at a later evening it was resolved to do both. So it was with the other proposals, resisted obstinately at first, but with steady, gentle persistence, the new Rector won his way.

View of Holy Trinity Church from Washbrooks Farm

The Reverend Cary Hampton Borrer ministered at Hurstpierpoint for fifty-seven years, and passed away in 1898. During his encumbency he was responsible not only for the building of Holy Trinity Church in 1845, but also:

1. Collaborating with the Reverend Nathaniel Woodard of Shoreham to found St John's College in 1849.
2. The building of the new Church of England Schools in Cuckfield Road on land given by Mr C. S. Hannington in 1868.
3. The building of Christ Church, Sayers Common, in 1880.
4. The building of the Hurstpierpoint Parish Room by Public Subscription in 1890.

Whilst in the parish he celebrated three jubilees – his golden wedding, the 50th anniversary of his institution to the living, and the 50th anniversary of the consecration of the church. His notable clerical career extended to six decades. Described in his obituary as a man of remarkable gentleness and sanctity of character, he had christened the larger number of parishioners, married most of them, and addressed nearly all of the village children by their Christian names, never passing one of them without a friendly word of greeting. He was respected by all, not least because his attitude to

The High Street – looking east. (Mr G. Stoner of the Lamb Inn filling the street water cart. The Drinking Fountain was a memorial to Mr Henry Holman, surgeon in the village for nearly 60 years.)

The High Street – looking west

working men and women was exactly the same as to those of his own social class. In her book, *Memories of Hurst*, which was published in 1975, Vivienne Manchester alludes to his good manners:

> He is still affectionately remembered by a few residents, who recall seeing this cheerful, elderly man in his latter years being wheeled in his wicker chair round the village by his sisters, always dressed in frock coat and top hat, and never shaking hands with a lady without first removing his glove.

But Mr Wood shall have the last word on describing the Reverend Borrer's courtesy:

> I well remember, as a raw youth of sixteen or seventeen, seeing the old gentleman about to enter the high wooden gate of the Rectory from the village street. Before he could do so, the gate opened from inside, one of the housemaids was just coming out, and stepped back when she saw the Rector, but he too stood back, raised his hat to her, and waited for her to pass before he entered himself. It made an impression on me that I have never forgotten.

Birds in Churches

The Church of Holy Trinity not only catered for the spiritual needs of the human inhabitants of Hurstpierpoint, but also served as a sanctuary for other creatures from the parish. In 1929 and 1930, the then curate, the Reverend Howard J. Emmet, wrote about a colony of jackdaws that had taken up residence in the belfry. His notes, which took the form of a calendar were published in the old *Sussex County Magazine* and some extracts from it are as follows:

> MARCH: nest building in earnest starts this month and sticks were dropped wholesale. The birds wasted quite as many as they used, if not more,and if you happened to be inside the Church when a stick dropped on it, you might think a stone had hit the roof. Nest building was mostly done in the morning and in between whiles the birds often indulged in short joy-flights. Sometimes it would be in a company when they would fly off together, chattering like a lot of schoolboys; sometimes in pairs with the cock turning and twisting as he pursued the hen in aerial courtship.
>
> APRIL: During the early part of April not only sticks were carried in but much other material with which to line the nests. A fair sample of what was used could be found at the foot of the tower. There were bits of newspaper, cabbage stalk, bread crusts, rag, rope, garden labels, a couple of clothes-pegs and a good amount of sheep's wool.
>
> There were nine nests in all, seven in the belfry lights and two higher up in the spire lights; and nine pairs of birds.

Shortly after his observations were published, the Reverend Emmet moved to Stoughton, and whilst there, submitted another article to the *Sussex County Magazine*, this time on birds that build in Sussex Churches. Referring again to the jackdaws, he said:

> One spring (1929) I found a nest actually built on one of the bells. Of course it came to grief, because the Sunday's ringing always upset it.

His list included starlings, barn owls (often referred to as church owls), swallows, (a pair of which regularly nested under the lych-gate), blue tits, house sparrows and the common pigeon. Finally there was the wren, and with regards to this tiny bird, the reverend gentleman said:

> For several years a pair of wrens built their nest inside one or the other of the hollow stone corbels that frame the windows at St. George's, Hurstpierpoint – a curious site.

The Reverend Emmett was a regular contributor to the *Sussex County Magazine*, and the substance of his articles not only dwelt with the behaviour of birds, but with that of his human flock as well. For instance, the following rather droll story tells of an occasion when a clergyman from Hurstpierpoint went to visit an old man who, although dying, was conscious up to the end. The sick man's bed had been brought down to the 'parlour' so as to save his wife the trouble of going up and down stairs in waiting on him. One day the Curate called and after a solemn talk with the old man, he noticed a fine ham on the sideboard upon which the invalid had his eyes. Presently the wife came into the sick chamber, and the paralytic said: "I would like a bit oo' that 'am; I would like it so much!" His wife ignored the remark at first. but when the poor old fellow reiterated his desire, she turned to him and said: "No, you can't have none o' that 'am; we're saving it up for your funeral!"

The Brighton Road – Looking south

Entente Cordiale!

That Hurstpierpoint is ancient is surely beyond dispute, and yet it has been strangely neglected by historians, for to the best of our knowledge, apart from village guide books, no truly definitive account has ever been written about the place. In *Mid Sussex through the Ages*, the author A. H. Gregory rather vaguely mentions that men from Hurst were at the Battle of Hastings, that they took part in the crusades to the Holy Land, and that they fought at Agincourt, but he gives no clear references to the sources of his information.

With regard to the more recent Napoleonic campaigns however, we are on firmer ground. Apparently 'Bonyparty', as he was commonly referred to in Sussex dialect, was as much feared as 'Old Nick' himself, and it was not a question of whether there would be an invasion – but when!

The oft-repeated cry, "The French be coming" was guaranteed to cause a panic, as was confirmed by Mr Charles Jenner, a butcher in nearby Cuckfield. He told of the alarm created early one morning in 1784, when the Prince of Wales, followed by some gentlemen (all on horseback) were seen riding at full gallop through the town. The local population assumed that the enemy had landed at Brighton, and that His Royal Highness was flying for his life! Of course it was nothing half so exciting, for it later transpired that the Prince, who had been enjoying high jinks with his cronies, had made a wager that he would ride to London and back via Cuckfield and Crawley in one day. Relays of fresh horses were provided every few miles, and he was said to have won the bet by performing the journey in four and a half hours going, and five and a half hours coming back.

But, incidents like this apart, the threat from France was taken very seriously indeed, and for several years to come, the Emperor cast a long shadow over Sussex. We have already alluded to the 'Troop of Horse' raised by William (2) Borrer of Pakyn's Manor. He was not alone in his actions, as was made abundantly clear by an unnamed Hurst diarist, who in November 1803, wrote:

> Volunteer corps of infantry are now formed all over the kingdom, and also of cavalry. Mr Campion of Danny, has a troop of horse, consisting of about forty men, young farmers principally. There is also a company of infantry in this parish of Hurst, about sixty men. Mr John Roberts is Captain. Also one at Keymer, Plumpton, Henfield etc. We expect a visit from the French daily. Waggons are getting ready to convey the women and children to different parts of the county nearer London. I understand the inhabitants between Lewes and Shoreham rivers are to go to Copthorne, St Leonard's Forest etc.

Then, speculating on the possibility of invasion, the diarist went on to state:

> Nobody doubts of their (the French) being defeated by sea or land, provided our men stand true. All party matters seem to be done away, and people are of one mind about the invasion, that is, nobody is afraid of them. Fire beacons of faggots and straw are set up on all the heights in the county. There is one on Wolstonbury, also on Chanctonbury, Cissbury and Hollingbury Hills, Crowborough and Leith Hills. These are guarded by three or four soldiers each, and in case the French should appear, they are to be fired in order to alarm the country.

Later, after referring to Napoleon's abdication in the spring of 1814, and the consequent peace in Europe, the chronicler proceeded:

> We have had great rejoicings at Hurst. Suspended a white flag above the top of the spire, consisting of forty-three yards of calico cut asunder so as to make two breadths, and being a strong wind to extend it, it had a good effect. All the principal inhabitants dined at the New Inn, and we collected twenty guineas for the poor. Mr Borrer gave another treat for them at West Town.

Baker's the Butchers-
Mr A. J. Baker in the doorway with daughter, Kitty. Brothers Alfred and Cecil are with pony and trap.

Southdown Tea Gardens – now Vinyard's Lodge

The New Inn

School Days

James Nye – he, who earlier in these pages, reminisced about former coaching days on the old London Road, also commented briefly on his education. He said:

> I was born in 1835 and went to Sayers Common School the first day it opened. Mrs Sharman was the school mistress. Afterwards I went to school in High Street, Hurst, kept by a Mr White. When I was a boy, the pupils often knew as much as their teachers.

His remarks are supported by Vivienne Manchester. In *Memories of Hurst*, she states that when St. Lawrence's school was opened in 1869, eighty-seven youngsters attended class and the headmaster was the only qualified teacher in the establishment. Obviously unable to do the job alone, he selected a number of brighter pupils to assist him, and gave them special training. For doing this, his salary was increased by an additional £4 per annum. More often than not, the extra tuition was given before lessons, as was shown by the school log, which recorded on April 17th, 1874, "began this week to take pupil teachers at 6.55am."

Vivienne Manchester goes on to say:

> Education not being compulsory in those days, attendances at school fluctuated considerably. There are many entries in the log book saying attendance was reduced through boys away haying, harvesting or acorning, and if the weather was bad, the children stayed at home. At the beginning of the 20th century, cleanliness and neatness were being strived for incessantly by the headmaster, and the following entries in the log book were seen many times:
>
> "B – sent home at 9am to clean boots, did not return. The same thing has happened before.
>
> There is a great improvement in the cleanliness of the boys, more collars and clean boots are seen every morning.
>
> A personal inspection of boots, hands, faces, ears is held before school every morning and afternoon.

Of all the schools that have ever been at Hurstpierpoint, St. John's College is surely the best known. It is one of a group – others in Sussex include Lancing and Ardingly – that have their origins in Shoreham, for it was there in 1847 that Nathaniel Woodard, a local curate, opened a small establishment in which to teach the sons of middle-class parents. So successful were his efforts that he conceived the idea of founding a series of schools designed to cater for the upper middle and lower middle classes. They were to be conducted on Church of England principles, and because he believed that "Education without religion is in itself a pure evil", each was dominated by its chapel. He desired to place them in positions where the buildings would show to best advantage, in order that masters and boys would draw continual inspiration from their environment. In his view, no system of education would be perfect which did not provide for the cultivation of the taste of the pupils through daily familiarity with the finest examples of architecture. Hurstpierpoint was the chosen site for the first of the middle schools, and the founder, who possessed a keen eye for natural beauty, spent considerable time exploring the district before deciding where the new school should be placed. That his choice was inspired is reflected in the words of Sabine Baring-Gould, the author of 'Onward Christian Soldiers', who served as a master during the early days of the college:

> Never have I seen such sunrises and sunsets as I did at Hurstpierpoint from the terrace. Many and many a time have I stood there and watched the glory of departing day. I looked and wondered...and I learned a great deal.

While plans were underway for the erection of the present buildings, Mansion House in the village was used as a temporary abode, and as such was opened in January, 1850. The following account of the occasion, written by Peter Woodard, the great-grandson of the Founder, and himself a former member of the college staff, appeared in the old *Sussex County Magazine* in 1950:

Hurstpierpoint a hundred years ago must have been a very pleasant, sleepy, country village. Instead of the long line of cars and lorries which pass through its narrow streets today, one would have only seen a farm cart or two, a couple of farmers' gigs, the doctor in his stanhope, or a barouche or victoria bearing a lady from one of the big houses on the outskirts. But on this particular day in January the village was very wide awake.The street, as we read in a contemporary account, was filled with people, many of them strangers brought by the railway to Hassocks Gate. Some walked, others rode; farmers and tradesmen exchanged views; a gentlemanly man with a boy in a handsome dog cart with a liveried servant was duly noted. All gradually converged on the Mansion House where the Treasurer awaited the payment of fees for the ensuing term. There seems to have been considerable confusion, some parents paying too much, others too little; others again into the wrong account. But eventually all was rectified and then the crowd moved down to the church, where a service was held. The sermon was preached by the Bishop of Chichester

Afterwards there was a luncheon party in the Market House which was "plentifully supplied". Apparently the boys of the school, thirty-four in number, were not invited, for they were observed to be making friends in the street, "rosy open country faces and sharp priggish-looking London children." Speeches followed the luncheon: then the crowd gradually dispersed and by five o'clock Hurst had returned to its normal state.

The ceremonial laying of the corner stone of the new school building took place in June, 1851, and in the words of Peter Woodard:

The occasion was made a general holiday in Hurst: triumphal arches were raised both in the village and at the approach to the new site, some of the brickwork was already up, there were plenty of flags and bunting in evidence, and a large assembly to greet the Bishop. The architect (Richard Carpenter) and his assistant were there with a silver trowel and a mason's mallet, this last being made from oak taken from the Chapel of the Royal Pavilion at Brighton.

Two years later, on 21st June 1853, the school was opened. It was the first Woodard school to obtain permanent buildings, and the first to present the founder's conception of artistic fitness and practical convenience. The style is Decorated Gothic, and the materials used are split flints and Caen stone.

Precious to the memory of many an old boy are the traditions, institutions and customs which are a source of pride and qualification and distinctive mark of Hurst. Charles Wyatt, who spent his formative years in the village, recalled how on Ascension Day, the college choir made a yearly pilgrimage to the site of the old Roman camp at the summit of Wolstonbury Hill, where, after a pause for breath, they sang hymns in Latin. There was also the popular 'Boar's Head' carol procession, and the annual Shakespeare play. Two performances were given, one for the parents, governors and honoured guests, the other for the villagers and after both there was a good repast.

This Shakespeare Society was founded as far back as 1854 by the first headmaster, Dr E. C. Lowe, and it is claimed to be the oldest school Shakespearean Society in the country. The earliest productions were staged with the distinguished assistance of the great Charles Keane, and the college society is numbered amongst those who contributed to his Testimonial in 1860.

As early as 1858 there were large attendances at the plays and as many as six hundred visitors crowded into the School Hall to see the first part of King Henry IV. While later on during the Victorian and Edwardian eras the audiences must have been exhausted by the time the carriages had arrived. For the occasion had been considerably lengthened by the old custom of orchestral interludes and glee-singing between acts. There was even an afterpiece. Until 1902,

St. John's College

the main course of the evening was often followed by such fare as 'Scenes from Pickwick', Aladdin', 'Cox and Box' etc. In consequence the theatre-goers frequently remained until one o'clock in the morning.

Sometimes drama was contained in drama, or at least, that was the experience of schoolmaster Sabine Baring-Gould:

> On one occasion (he wrote) we performed Macbeth. A cauldron was improvised of black glazed calico, with a metal tray going half round the interior, on which were placed sundry fireworks, and I in my dress-suit was seated cross-legged in the midst of the cauldron. My function was to ignite the fireworks as the witches danced round the vessel. 'Bubble, bubble, toil and trouble' was my catchword for a big display. And a big display was effected by setting fire to a flower-pot' as a certain explosive and showery firework is called by pyrotechnists. When the first witch sang:
>
> > 'Round about the cauldron go;
> > In the poisoned entrails throw.'
>
> I sent up a flame of strontium, that spread a crimson glow over everything.
>
> > Toad, that under the cold stone
> > Days and nights hast thirty-one
> > Sweltered venom sleeping got,
> > Boil thou first i' the charmed pot.'
>
> Up started green flame. But then came the revolution about the cauldron, and my cue for the flower-pot, which was on the ledge of the cauldron-ring. All I had to do was apply the match. This I did, and away went the witches and demons dancing round the vessel. But the vibration of the stage, caused by their feet upset the flower-pot outside the cauldron. Thereupon one of the witches caught it up and without thinking that I was in the vessel, threw the roaring, hissing, spluttering and blazing firework upon me. Down went the curtain, and Mrs Lowe, with admirable presence of mind, rushed onto the stage and enveloped me in the warm woollen mantle she had happily brought with her. I was not hurt, but my dress-suit was riddled and my small clothes especially exhibited a point-lace consistency.

PC Edgeler

While engaged in the task of research, we had the rare opportunity of examining the Day Book that had been kept in the front office at Hurstpierpoint police station during the early years of the Twentieth Century (1906 to 1910). As a historical document it was worth its weight in gold, for the entries, beautifully recorded in copper-plate handwriting, dealt with the everyday life of the village and described in great detail, the duties and responsibilities of the men whose job it was to keep the peace.

It revealed for instance, that apart from the time off in lieu of sickness or annual leave, officers were actually on duty for at least ten to eleven hours each day, every day of the year, and as bicycles were not generally available, patrols were normally conducted on foot, with approximately twelve miles a day being covered in the process.

For example; it is recorded that on Saturday, 23-2-1907, PC Edgeler, who was recently posted from Hassocks, left Hurstpierpoint at 9.30am and walked to Saddlescombe where he spoke to the farmer, Mr Robinson, about dog licence exemptions. From there he walked to the Plough Inn at Pyecombe to discuss a similar matter with the landlord, Mr Godley, after which he returned to Hurstpierpoint and booked off at 3.30pm. He booked on again at 8pm, and during a general round of the village, sought from those who might know, information concerning a recent theft of copper. He finally booked off at midnight, having worked ten hours and walked twelve miles. On another occasion he walked to Handcross, where assisted by the local policeman, a Constable Pilbeam, he performed what was described as; 'Special duty-timing motorists'. The two men then walked to Staplefield to repeat the exercise there, and upon completing the stint, returned to their respective homes. PC Edgeler who arrived back at Hurstpierpoint at 9pm, had been on continual duty for thirteen and a half hours that day, in which time he had walked a total of twenty-two miles.

Timing motorists was his speciality and the ability was seemingly recognised by the force hierarchy, for the record indicates that he was required to travel (although presumably not on foot) and operate at places as far distant as Northiam and Battle. Mountfield and Newhaven, and even Hastings and Rye. Thus the Hurstpierpoint policeman's face, became a familiar, if not exactly popular, sight throughout the county.

While motoring transgressions were becoming an increasing burden, the Day Book shows that the greatest portion of police time was devoted to enforcing legislation relating to rural matters. Gipsies had to be continually moved on, animal licences had to be regularly checked, and many other procedures, such as sheep-dipping, or the destruction of diseased livestock had to be officially witnessed. In addition to which, the village constable was very much at the disposal of the lord of the manor and other dignitaries. In essence this meant, that should say, a function be held at the residence of one of these worthies, the policeman was expected to show his face and keep a discreet eye on the proceedings. 'To be seen, but not heard', as the saying goes.

An example of this is nicely illustrated in the Day Book. Commencing on the 7-12-1908, it shows that PC Edgeler, who had already completed an early morning tour of duty, booked on again at

William James Edgeler (retirement photograph)

11pm and worked through the night until 7.15am, most of which time he was guarding wedding presents at Danny House. And that was not the end of the matter, for after returning to duty at 11.30am and completing a three and a half hour patrol of the village, he booked on once more at 5.30pm, this time for a straight shift of thirteen hours, the bulk of which were again spent at Danny watching over the presents. In all, PC Edgeler had worked a total of twenty-eight and three-quarters hours during a thirty-two and a half hour period, most of which had been spent in the capacity of nightwatchman for the local squire.

However, lest any reader form the wrong impression, it should be pointed out that PC Edgeler was no 'rich-man's lackey' as was demonstrated shortly after these all-night vigils when, probably feeling disgruntled from lack of sleep, he reported a Lady Mary Chayter for not possessing a dog licence, and whilst about it, he reported the vicar as well.

Before the First World War, little serious crime was recorded in the district but when it did occur, it was dealt with the utmost severity. For instance, if found guilty of nearly any form of theft, the culprit would certainly face the prospect of imprisonment, although magistrates occasionally exercised discretion. An example of this was the case of a Hurstpierpoint lad who appeared before the bench charged with stealing a silk wrap. Because of his tender years, the youth was given the option of either going to prison or enlisting in the navy. He opted for the latter, and as a result was taken by police escort to Purfleet in Essex, where he was handed over to the commanding officer of HMS Cornwall, a government training establishment alongside the River Thames.

Inspector Turner Edgeler

Burglary was rare indeed, and if committed received every attention. A case in point occurred in nearby Hassocks, when two ladies returning home, were unexpectedly confronted by a strange man who emerged from their house and fled down the road. They then discovered that the premises had been forcibly entered and ransacked and property of considerable value was missing. By a stroke of good fortune, PC Edgeler, was covering the area for a sick colleague and happened to be passing by. Upon receipt of the complaint, he conducted an immediate search of the neighbourhood,and greatly to his credit, found the felon. What happened next is contained in an extract from the court proceedings as published by the *Mid Sussex Times.*

> PC Edgeler spoke to searching for the prisoner, and to finding him concealed in some bushes at Hassocks about a quarter of a mile from the house of the prosecutrix. He told him he believed he was the man he was looking for – for taking some stuff in Woodsland Road,and the prisoner replied; "Yes, it's a fair cop, I'll go quiet if you are not rough." In his possession he had some of the stolen things, and when charged at Haywards Heath, he said: "You have got the right one."

After the hearing, the prisoner, described as an incorrigible rogue who had unsuccessfully tried to implicate others into the affair, was sentenced (quite leniently many considered) to three years hard labour.

In what must be a near unique record, four succeeding generations of the Edgeler family have served in the police. The first to be appointed was Mr Turner Edgeler, a fine amateur cricketer who was an Inspector in the Surrey force. His son, James Turner Edgeler (of whom we have written) joined the neighbouring East Sussex Constabulary, and retired at the rank of Superintendent. His son, Sergeant Bill Edgeler (also of the East Sussex Constabulary) was a widely respected and enormously popular officer, as was his son, PC Terry Edgeler, who spent several years as a resident village constable at Ardingly.

Sergeant Bill Edgeler

PC Terry Edgeler with Mark Dudeney

The Road to Uganda

At the eastern end of the High Street stands an imposing mansion called St. George's. It is of considerable age, and during the 1840s was purchased by a wealthy Brighton shopkeeper named Charles Smith Hannington. His children were born there and he resided at the premises for the rest of his life. In so doing, his story, and that of his son, James, has become so woven into the history of Hurstpierpoint, that no account of the village could be considered complete without reference to it.

It all started when Charles as a lad, entered the family's retailing business and swiftly displayed a natural aptitude for the work. However, he also possessed military aspirations and his father, not wishing to lose the services of his son, wisely suggested that he might consider joining up as a part-time volunteer in the Brighton Coastal Battery. This the youngster did, and the experience he gained, gave him great satisfaction. Then, following the unit's eventual closure, he transferred to the local corps of the Sussex Volunteer Artillery, with equally gratifying results.

In due course he married and at about this time moved to the aforementioned St George's at Hurstpierpoint, and there, despite matrimonial obligations and an increasing involvement in commerce, his enthusiasm for the volunteers remained undiminished. He was still actively engaged when three of his own sons, Samuel, Philip and James enlisted in the Corps. The first two boys rose to captain, and James to Lieutenant, while in 1868, Charles himself was made commanding officer. It was a deserved promotion for he had done much for the advancement of the service, and was popular with the men. Indeed, he never lost their affection, as was demonstrated long after his retirement when the Regimental band frequently turned up at their old Colonel's home and played for his enjoyment.

Several years earlier, and for reasons we have been unable to establish, Charles had a difference of opinion with the Reverend Cary Hampton Borrer, which was at once so bitter and acrimonious, that even that celebrated peace-maker was unable to repair the rift. The consequence being that Charles made an oath never to enter the

Parish church again. He resolved instead to build a place of worship on his own land, which is precisely what he did, and a small flint-walled church built in mock-Gothic style was erected in his grounds. Called St. George's Church, but known originally as Little Park Chapel, it was not recognised by the Church of England, and so only non-conformist services could be held there. But happily, time heals, and in 1867, fifteen years after the angry words were spoken the antagonists made up, and all was forgiven if not forgotten. A licence for worship was granted by the Bishop of Chichester, and what had been a ministry of dissent was consecrated as a Chapel of Ease.

St. George's Church (The bell tower has since been removed as it was considered to be dangerous)

Shortly before the event occurred, James Hannington, Charles' youngest son, wrote the following words in his diary:

> Sunday, October 26th, 1867 – Mr Hart preached the farewell sermon with a good bit of true emotion. I was the only member of the family there, and gave the old man ten shillings as a present. My liberal father pensions him off at £50 a year, and he was after all, not the stated minister, only a supply who came frequently and had nothing else to depend on.

At this stage of his development, James – who clearly felt at home in the chapel's atmosphere – had experienced a comfortable upbringing and was given free rein to cultivate his interests. They, apart from the Volunteers, included such diverse pursuits as collecting and categorising wild flowers, yachting, and foreign travel. He worked in his father's store, it is true, but with little enthusiasm, and his character, according to R. Whybrow, in an article published in the *Sussex County Magazine* was :

> ...too unusual and erratic to conform to the limitations of a business life. The Chapel in the grounds of St George's brought him in closer touch with churchmen than he had ever been before, and he was seized with the desire to take orders, although he looked at it more as an escape than a call.

Whybrow's comments are confirmed by the following entry made in James' diary in 1868:

> I had it fixed in my mind that I was to be ordained, but for real motives – I had none.

It was in this state of uncertainty that he eventually proceeded to Oxford, where by all accounts he became a great favourite, and a great sportsman – but hardly a satisfactory student. However he succeeded in his object and was duly ordained in 1874, after which he obtained the living of Martinhoe in Devon. It proved to be shortlived, for just a few months later he returned to Sussex and took charge of the Chapel at Hurstpierpoint, which his father now offered him. A boy had left, and a man returned, for in his absence his mother had died, and her loss proved to have a maturing and sobering effect on his personality. Whybrow remarked:

> Men crowded to his services, where they heard the plain truth about themselves.

Whether such frankness endeared James to his congregation is not reported, but the local children certainly liked him. Apparently he rarely walked down the street without a pocketful of bullseyes to distribute amongst them. He was surely the clergyman that Bessie Wooler referred to in an article about her childhood that was published many years ago in the *Mid Sussex Times*. Describing the aftermath of an outing to the famous Chinese Gardens, she wrote:

> Then we sat down to tea, and afterwards, the rector who had come in his dogcart with his groom, threw a large bag of sweets on the grass, and we scrambled for them – sweets were scarce then.

Travel had always been James' greatest passion, and taking holy orders in no way affected this. In a move obviously designed to mix business with pleasure, he set about persuading the ecclesiastical authorities that missionary work was his true vocation. And he would seem to have put up a good case, for in just a few years he had sailed to Africa. What he expected to find there we can only guess. What he did find was disease, suffering, and unrelenting hardship. His task it would appear was to create a missionary trail from Zanzibar to the interior, and then on to Lake Nyanza in Uganda. Whybrow's comments on the undertaking make depressing reading:

> The story of the first journey presents a picture of grim determination in the face of every kind of obstacle, for hundreds of miles – mosquitoes, fever, swamps, rivers, wild beasts forest and desert. Though dogged by constant illness, he (James) plodded on, the life and soul of the caravan, a miracle of endurance.

But Hannington had his limitations, he was only a man and a sick one at that, and although his spirit was undaunted, he was unable to complete the journey and returned to England instead. A few

James Hannington

months at home did wonders for his health, and before long he was cured of his ailments – but not from his longing to return to Africa. In an amazingly short time he had developed an intense love of the place, and although it had treated him badly, he wished more than anything else to return,and plant the standard of the cross where it had never been set before. The Church Missionary Society were convinced that he was the man for the job, so they sent him back again, this time plus apron and gaiters – The Bishop of Eastern Equatorial Africa.

More determined than ever to reach Lake Nyanza, he planned a new course, this time by an upland route. It would be six weeks shorter and far more healthy for Europeans, and he hoped to create a chain of Mission Stations along the way. So the journey started, and though beset by wild beasts, deserted by carriers, and threatened by starvation, they carried on. His judgement was proved to be correct, the way was far superior to the other, but then, without warning, tragedy struck!

In the mistaken belief that he was in friendly territory, the Bishop had pushed on to within sight of the Nile, when his small party was ambushed by hostile tribesmen. They were marched into captivity, tortured and humiliated, then about a week later, taken to a lonely spot in the forest, and brutally speared to death.

A monument marks the spot where James stood on that fateful day. He was still a young man of thirty-eight, and known only among a small circle of acquaintances and friends, yet his murder and that of his companions in 1885, has made him in the words of Whybrow:

> One of an immortal band, of the thread of whose lives is woven the fabric of our national character.

Tucked out of sight from passers-by, St. George's Church at Hurstpierpoint, the creation of Charles Smith Hannington, still stands. On the wall within, a black slate tablet commemorates his fourth son, James Hannington D.D. former curate of the Chapel, First Bishop of East Equatorial Africa, and the man who purchased the road to Uganda with his life.

Thomas Marchant

There are few more reliable records on which to base an estimate of domestic life and manners of any given period than the casual and outspoken entries of a diary-writer. Sussex has been particularly favoured in this respect as several of its natives have left behind them diaries which present us with a true picture of the lives of our ancestors in the seventeenth and eighteenth centuries. The Rev. Giles Moore, Rector of Horsted Keynes was one. Timothy Burrell of Cuckfield, another. In addition there was Squire Stapley of Hickstead Place, Thomas Turner of East Hoathly, Walter Gale of Mayfield, John Burgess of Ditchling and Thomas Marchant, a farmer from Hurstpierpoint.

Marchant began his journal in 1714. He was an English yeoman, and his home at Little Park was a house of some pretensions, nearly ranking alongside Danny, Pakyn's Manor and Randolf's Farm in age and historical significance. He farmed extensively and also bought and sold fresh water fish in large quantities, as is indicated by the following entry:

> We took 242 fish out of the stew[1] for Mr Edmead. Received £10 of Richard Baldchild for them. They were, one with another, about 13" long.

[1] A pond for keeping fish for eating

The diary contains many references to stock-breeding, general purchases, and the fattening of pigs. But other items are mentioned as well, a cricket match for instance, the erection of a "singing gallery" in the parish church, and the arrival of a dancing master at the village. The writer was also extremely proud of an acquisition described as "a case to carry pen and ink and sand".

It is interesting to note that contrary to many modern accounts of those times, all of the diarists we have alluded to, reveal striking evidence not only of the absence of social distinctions, but of the prevailing friendly intercourse that existed between the classes. Marchant, for example, although only a yeoman farmer, and at one time steward to the Duke of Somerset at Petworth, mixed on terms of equality with everyone, including the landed gentry, with whom he supped and dined regularly. A little too regularly perhaps, for it was after a visit to Danny that he recorded the well known and often quoted observation, "staid late and drunk too much". But obviously not deterred by over-indulgence, he wrote on another occasion:

> After evening prayer, Mr Campion, Mr Hay, Mr Bateman, the Frenchman (Unidentified), Mr Hart and I, went to Mr Whitpaine's at West-towne, where we drank three bottles of beer and a small bowl of punch.

The pleasures of the table are also described:

> We had a trout for supper, two feet, two inches long from eye to fork, and six inches broad; it weighed ten and a half pounds. It was caught in the Albourne brook, near Trussell House...

And should any reader think this entry sounds somewhat incomplete Marchant concludes with a variation of his remark: "We staid very late and drank enough".

Little Park Farm (The pond was known as the Wilderness)

There was a time many years ago (but long after Thomas Marchant's residency), when a sports day was held every August Bank Holiday on land at Little Park Farm, and one villager, reminiscing about the "great days" before the First World War recalled:

> The Home Field at the rear of St. Lawrence's School was the venue. It was lent by Mr Sam Tobbitt, who was the farm tenant then. With the ancient house and St. John's College so prominently in the background the place was a marvellous setting for spectator and competitor alike. The grandstand consisted of hay wagons, lined up and roped off, and anyone wishing to take advantage of the facility was charged a shilling for the privilege. The event was always well attended with participants coming from far and wide.Their numbers invariably including the famous Arthur Shrubb, a champion long-distance runner who seemed to harbour a special affection for Hurstpierpoint, for he competed every year and never failed to win.

Poynings Southdown Band (playing in St. John's Park, Burgess Hill)

> During the intervals between the races, either the Hurstpierpoint Town Band, or the Poynings Southdown Band played musical selections, while a clown named Whimsical Walker entertained the onlookers.
>
> The undoubted highlights of the meeting were the horse and pony races organised by Mr Horace Broad of Ham Farm. Hurdles were erected in strategic positions round the field, and a pond in the middle was used as a water jump. Many a jockey ended up in there, including Horace on occasion, but he was a great favourite, and usually the first to pass the winning post.

Danny House and the Campions

There are surely few more delightful sights than that of the mansion of Danny, when viewed from the slopes of Wolstonbury Hill. Built of brick in the classical Elizabethan style, with numerous bay windows to the front, it is the very epitome of an English country residence. Horsfield, in his *History of Sussex* states that the present building was erected in 1595 by George Goring, who thirteen years earlier in 1582, purchased the lordship and estate from Gregory, Lord Dacre. He goes on to say that Goring was knighted by James 1 in 1608, and in 1648, during the English Civil War, was in command at Colchester, where after a siege lasting ten weeks, he surrendered to the parliamentary forces.

Can Horsfield be right? If he is, sixty-six years would have elapsed between the time of Goring's arrival at Hurst and his participation in the siege. There appears to be no record of his age when he acquired Danny, so if we assume he was twenty-five, he would have been ninety-one whilst defending the garrison, and that, with respect, seems an unlikely state of affairs.

In an attempt to shed some light on the matter, we turned to *The Worthies of Sussex* by Mark Anthony Lower, and he had this to say:

The second son of Sir William Goring of Burton, who died in 1553, founded the branch of the family who settled at Ovingdean, Lewes and Hurstpierpoint, and who built the mansion at Danny. This branch produced the celebrated Sir George Goring, who was elevated to the peerage by Charles 1 in 1632, as Baron Goring of Hurstpierpoint and appointed to several high offices. He took an active part in the Royalist cause, and was for his services, advanced to the Earldom of Norwich. At the siege of Colchester, which lasted ten weeks, he was chief-in-command, but was compelled on August 28, 1648 to surrender to Lord Fairfax.

There we appear to have it, for although Lower is not entirely specific, he does state that a son of Sir William Goring built the mansion, and it was *this branch* that produced a descendant who fought for the king. All of which helps to confirm our view that the George Goring who first resided at Danny was not, as Horsfield seems to suggest, George Goring, the defender of Colchester, but his father.

As a footnote, it is a strange but interesting coincidence that amongst those who fell at the siege of Colchester was a Sir William Campion, whose family at a future date were destined to become the proprietors of Danny.

In 1652, Danny became the property of Peter Courthope, and when he died without male issue, his daughter, Barbara, became heiress to the estate. She was married to Henry Campion of Combwell in Kent, and in 1728, three years after her father's death, the couple made Danny their home, and the family has retained the Lordship of the manor ever since.

Henry died on April 14th, 1761, and a tablet to his memory can be seen in the Campion Chapel at Holy Trinity Church, Hurstpierpoint. As may be expected, it extols his virtues to the full, which makes it much too lengthy to include here. But what we will reproduce is an elegy (the only clue to the authorship being the initials, T.P.) that on June 15th, 1761, appeared in the *Sussex Weekly Advertiser*, the first local newspaper to be printed in the county.

> Go mourn, thou Hurst! Thy joys are fled,
> The good, the Pious Campion's dead;
> Go mourn, ye Poor! Your loss is great,
> Your loss of Cloths, of Bread, of meat,
> Your Belly filled, nor was he slack,
> from Winter's cold to fence the Back;
> He like the Sun, diffused his heat
> To all around both small and great;
> A Friend to all, for all by him were fed,
> The Rich with Wisdom, and the poor with Bread.
> Then rest, Brave soul! and may thy memory be,
> Fragrant to all, as it is sweet to me.

Though quaintly phrased, the warmth and sincerity of the sentiments are obvious, and they reflect the loyalty and near bond that the large majority of villagers have always felt for the Campion family. In days gone by, the attitude of the populace to the residents of Danny was positively feudal. We mentioned earlier about the village policemen guarding wedding presents. Another example appeared in a delightful book published by Hurstpierpoint Women's Institute. Entitled *Village Memories,* it contained the following little gem:

> Someone remembers an old farm labourer being asked about his vote, and he said – "I ain't 'ad no orders, t'squire always takes us to the place and tells us what to do" – the squire being Colonel Campion.

More evidence of local regard can be found in an article printed in the *Mid Sussex Times* on the 14th January, 1908. Dealing with the return from Australia of the Reverend F. H. Campion[1] and his newly wedded wife, it stated that "Danny was the scene of great rejoicing last Tuesday evening." It went on to say that after disembarking from the train at Hassocks, the happy couple were conveyed home and,

> On their carriage arriving at the Sandfield Pond mid-way through the park, it was met by the estate

[1] A missionary son of Colonel Campion.

Hassocks Road, Hurstpierpoint, at the junction of New Way Lane

> servants, the Hurstpierpoint Fire Brigade, and a number of townspeople bearing lighted torches. The horses having been removed, the carriage was drawn by willing hands to the mansion, the torches having a striking effect as the procession passed along the avenue.

The Reverend Campion's father, Colonel William Henry Campion, CB, JP of Danny, was born on April 1st, 1836. He was the son of Mr W. J. Campion, JP and Harriet Campion neé Kemp, the daughter of Mr T. R. Kemp, the founder of Kemp Town, Brighton. Destined for the army, Colonel Campion served in the Crimea and then in the Indian Mutiny Campaign, 1857-8. He was in the 72nd Highlanders (later to become the Seaforth Highlanders) and was present at the siege of Kotah. He also took part in the famous pursuit of the rebel leaders, Tantora Topee and Rae Sahib.

His military career ended upon the accession to the squiredom of Danny, following his father's death in 1869. In his capacity as Lord of the Manor, Colonel Campion was, according to A. H. Gregory in *Mid Sussex Through the Ages*

> ....a good landlord (the chief landowner in the Hurst district) and a fine type of English country gentleman. At one period owning 3000 acres in Sussex.

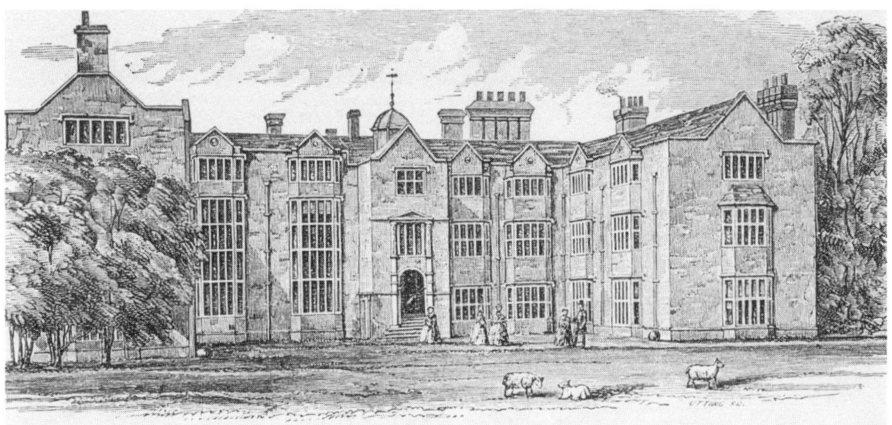

Danny House from an engraving by Utting

Meet of the Southdown Hunt at Danny

Little Danny (The Home Farm)

Upon his return he married Miss Gertrude Brand, whose father, the Right Hon H. B. W. Brand was a Speaker of the House of Commons. The young Mrs Campion was a lady with a strong social conscience, as was demonstrated in 1884 when she became the founder and president of a home for training workhouse girls in the skills of domestic service. In *Memories of Hurst*, Vivienne Manchester records:

> Elderly residents of Hurst still remember these girls in their quaint ankle-length cloaks with bonnets or straw hats, striped dresses in blue and white, blue stockings and boots. With their short cropped hair, they gave an impression of severeness and regimentation, particularly as they always walked in twos, whether it be to school or church.

Mrs Campion also had much to do with the founding of a convalescence establishment in Hurstpierpoint for women and children. Her husband donated an estate cottage for the purpose, and because of the premises' idyllic rural location, it became known as the Sunshine Home. In due course it was thought that the place should have a chapel. Work started on the project in 1913, and on the 29th April that year, Princess Alexander of Teck (the mother of Queen Mary) laid the foundation stone. The presence of the royal visitor had a stunning effect on the district, and the *Mid Sussex Times* in an extremely wordy report on the event, waxed quite lyrical. What follows is just a brief extract:

> People put out their decorations and poured out of their houses to greet the handsome Princess. It was St. George's Day. It was a Royal Day! It was a Sunshine Day – From lofty mansion to lowly cottage, the flags of Old England flew – The High Street was aglow with colour, ensignia and standards, pennants and streamers, spanned far over the winding roadway, line after line of them. Every preparation had been made to give a royal welcome to the good Princess.

And a royal welcome she certainly received. After arriving at Hassocks by train, the distinguished lady was transported to Hurst via Stonepound and Burgess Hill, thereby entering the village on the Cuckfield Road. Then, running the gauntlet of the cheering, flag-waving crowds, she was driven to Danny for lunch.

The ceremony was due to be held in the afternoon. A carpet had been laid in preparation, and as the appointed hour approached, members of the local Fire Brigade were posted either side of the pathway leading to the Home. The inmates, in their blue aprons were all lined up, as were a combined choir from Holy Trinity and St. George's Churches, while onlookers crowded into every available space, some even climbing onto the roof.

At 3.30pm the entourage arrived, and after a short service by the Bishop of Chichester, Colonel Campion handed the Princess a silver trowel with which she spread the mortar below the stone, and this, being suspended by chains, was then lowered into position.

Following numerous speeches and presentations, the Royal party left the Home, and amid rapturous applause, were driven back to Hassocks where they boarded a fast train that had ben specially stopped for them.

"Everything", in the words of the *Mid Sussex Times*, "passed off most happily and successfully."

Mrs Campion died in 1927, and Colonel Campion in 1928. The inheritance then passed to their son, Sir William Robert Campion, DSO, who earned his decoration when commanding a Sussex battalion in the First World War. Later he sat as Member of Parliament for Lewes, and at the time of his father's death, was the Governor of Western Australia.

Left to right: The Hon Mrs G. Campion – Princess Alexander of Teck, Col W. H. Campion, Lady Chaytor, The Bishop of Lewes, Reverend C. A. Marona, Rector of Hurstpierpoint

On his return to Danny, there was no side of life in the county – religion, education, the magistrate's bench, military training, scouting, sport – to which he did not render wholehearted service.

His wife (Lady Campion) whose grandfather succeeded the 'bad' Lord Byron in the peerage, also devoted herself to public affairs, being amongst other things, Chairman of the New Sussex Hospital

Sir William and Lady Campion opening the Ditchling Gooseberry Show

for Women, and the Deputy President of the Lewes Division of the British Red Cross Society. Sir William is remembered as a friendly man with a constant sense of humour that made him popular wherever he went. He died in 1951, and in an obituary that was published in the *Sussex County Magazine*. the writer said:

> His quiet sense of fun was always bubbling up. Once he described his march to the Rhine in 1918 at the head of his battalion: "Always marched at the head of them when we moved off in the morning – good thing for them to see the old man there – then they don't think he was canned the night before."

Sir William was succeeded by his son, Simon Campion, and then by his grandson, the late David Campion, who was the last of seven generations of the family to have lived at Danny. They have gone now, but the mansion remains, a historic link with Tudor Sussex, and an imperishable reminder to those who have resided there.

Hassocks Road, Hurstpierpoint. The white-fronted building at the junction with College Lane was called Lynton House, and in the years prior to its demolition, was a Reform School

Wolstonbury Hill: the grassy hollow just above the tree-line was known as 'Solomon's Gardens', while the two clumps of bushes close to the top of the hill were called, 'Campion's eyebrows'!

Opposite:
Belmont School, Clayton Wickham: Commanding a fine position at the foot of Belmont Lane, this old Georgian style mansion was originally the home of a retired Indian Army Officer. During the 1920s it underwent a chamge of use, being converted and extended into a Boy's Preparatory School for scholarships and entrance to the Public Schools and Royal Navy. It closed in the late 1950s and remained empty and neglected for many years. Then, because of its ruinous condition, the place was demolished and a dwelling resembling a pyramid was erected on the site.

Hassocks Road

Hassocks

The Broads of Ham Farm ~ Hassocks Station and its Approaches ~ Hassocks Wood ~ Spitalford Bridge, Hassocks School and the Herring Stream ~ Dale House and Hassocks Cinema ~ Wilmington Lodge, The Adastra Park and the Stafford family ~ The Box Brothers of Parkside

Heading east from Hurstpierpoint we come to the Ham, an ancient farmhouse that stands close to Buttinghill. It is part of the Danny estate and for many years was associated with the Broad family, two generations of which were tenant farmers there. The first of these, Mr Richard Broad, came to Mid Sussex in 1856, when he opened what was to swiftly become a flourishing butcher's shop situated near to Hurstpierpoint Church. In due course he handed the business over to one of his sons, while he went into farming on quite a large scale. At different times he was the tenant at Tott Farm, Locks Farm, Langton Farm, a farm at Burgess Hill, one or two others and finally, Ham Farm.At the Christmas fat stock shows, his name regularly appeared amongst the prize winners, and he was also among the prime movers in the former Hurstpierpoint 'Harvest Home' celebrations, when farmers and their men dined together after the crops had been gathered in. Mr Broad, who sat at the head of the long table, had a cheerful word and a smile for everyone. By all accounts he also had a fine voice, and on such occasions it took little prompting for him to sing his favourite song, which was 'The Farmer's Boy'.

Ham Farm

He died in 1908, and his passing, recorded in typical journalese of the time, read as follows:

> The wind moaned over the well kept farmery down in the fair vale of the Ham at Hassocks. Sheep were lowly bleating in a flood of sunshine on the eastern fold. The fine old farmhouse peeped up coolly from amid the greenery of the trees and shrubs. Cattle stood browsing on the hillock behind it. The sweet smell of new mown hay was wafted over the countryside; but the haymaking in the fields had for a time ceased. Quietude and rest were the impressions given by a striking Sussex landscape. The farm employees gathered, with faces sad and clothes dark, to form a sorrowing group on the lawn, for the Angel of Death had been reaping at the Ham, and Richard Broad, one of those cheery, good-hearted farmers, who lived a long life well, had been called to the great Harvest home.

To return to the subject of singing, Mr Broad was not alone in possessing this talent. Most villages of byegone days had their own particular songsters, both men and women. The men generally did their best at the local inn sing-songs. accompanied by a fiddle or a clarionet, and sometimes by the hand-bell ringers. The ploughing scene was often the theme of their song. Two famous village singers at one time were Bill Gander and Abraham Lewry, both of

Hurstpierpoint. Bill was carter to Mr Horace Broad (son of Richard) and Abraham was a local woodcutter and sheep shearer. One of their songs went something like this:

> He sat down on his plough to whistle and to sing
> And charmed the squire's daughter
> Who was nutting in the wood...
> He held her by the waist and gently sat her down.
> "Dear John," said she, "I think I see
> The world go round and round."

Hassocks Station and its Approaches

Before the first train steamed through Hassocks in 1840 or thereabouts, no village as such existed. The area was little more than woods and common land through which a sandy lane linked Hurstpierpoint with Keymer. East of Stonepound the route was very different to that used now. In those days it would have headed up and over what we refer to as Northbank and Station Approach West, then descended to the point where at a future date, the junction of Woodsland Road and Keymer Road was destined to appear. After the track was laid, a level crossing catered for the east to west traffic, but this was abolished approximately forty years later when the cutting containing the present highway and bridge was constructed.

Mention of the railway brings us back to James Nye, whose contributions concerning schooldays at Sayers Common and coaching on the London Road, appeared earlier in this book. With regards to the Brighton Line, he had this to say:

> I remember the making of the railway, which gradually stopped coaching. I saw as many as sixteen horses to one huge wagon on the king's highway, drawing wheelbarrows, picks, muck wagons and all sorts of things for the making of Clayton Tunnel.
>
> My father had me over at Hassocks to peep through the palings to see one of the first trains go by. The carriages were only open wagons.

The reason for building a railway station at such a lonely and uninhabited spot, has never to the best of our knowledge been fully established, but it might well have occurred because geographically speaking, the location was ideally suited for the loading and transportation of the famous Southdown sheep that grazed in large flocks on the nearby hills. There were certainly sidings for cattle trucks situated at the northern end of the station from an early date, and in an adjacent market yard, well attended livestock sales were held on alternate Thursdays throughout the year, while each December it was the venue for a Christmas fat stock show.

In 1881, the station was extended southwards, and new offices waiting rooms, and a station master's house were erected on the site of the former level crossing. The original building designed by the architect, David Mocatta, remained, but only in the capacity of a cottage. The goods yard at the southern end contained a coal wharf, an engine turntable, and extensive sidings that were used for marshalling freight trains to and from different parts of the Sussex coast, while a spur line branched off to Hudson sandpit which lay to the west of Stonepound.

With its mock Tudor façade, the new premises was pleasing to the eye and practical in concept. The unusually wide platforms were covered by canopies, thus affording protection from inclement weather, while during the winter months, the waiting rooms were heated by open coal fires, memories of which are still fondly recalled by senior members of the community. Sadly, memories are all they will ever be, for in an act of monumental folly, the authorities first allowed the fine old building to fall into disrepair, then demolished it, and few people who look at the bleak and windswept structure that stands in its place will ever understand why!

As a brief aside, it is worth recording that the station master was also the first postmaster in the village, and anyone wishing to despatch parcels or purchase stamps, did so from a wooden kiosk on the platform. However, it was hardly a practical arrangement, and in due course the business moved elsewhere.

The cutting with a slip road leading to Station Approach west

In those far off days, the west side of the railway station was the commercial heart of the village. It is hardly so now, but a reminder of past times may be gained by glancing at a tablet mounted high on the wall of the shop on the Hurst side of Stanford Avenue. The initials C.T. are clearly visible, and they refer to Charles Tully, who built the place as a grocery and general stores for his daughter Patience, and her husband Israel Avery. A few years earlier in 1891, the young couple had opened a grocer's shop just across the road at number 3 Stanford Terrace, and it was there after they left, that the Post Office transferred its operations.

Charles Tully also built Yeoman House in Stanford Avenue, and that is where he spent the last years of his life. He was in every respect a 'self-made' man, having risen from near obscurity to a position of influence in the community. Born at Scotches Farm near Burgess Hill, he was still only a baby when his mother committed suicide by drowning herself in the mill pond. As a result, the little fellow was raised by his grandparents, but upon reaching the age of thirteen, ran away from home to gain employment as a butcher's boy in Brighton. That he worked hard is demonstrated by the fact that in a few years he returned to Burgess Hill to run his own butchery business. Not content with that, he branched out into farming and in due course became a prosperous pig and sheep breeder, holding about two thousand acres of land at Poynings and Pangdean (where he resided for many years). In addition he acquired considerable house property at Burgess Hill, Hurstpierpoint, East Grinstead, Hassocks and Brighton, and also went in for building.

To have earned the respect of one's peers, is an acolade all desire but few obtain, and in a passage from his book, *A Sussex Farmer,* William Wood accords such tribute to Charles Tulley. While discussing the poor quality of the sheep exhibited at Lindfield Fair during a particularly dry year, he had this to say:

> I came across a rather large consignment of both ewes and lambs quite up to the standard of better seasons. The owner, Mr Chas. Tulley of Pangdean Farm, sat on the wattles, and I congratulated him upon the fact that his sheep were as good as they always had been in spite of the drought. "Yes," he said, "nine years out of ten my flock keeps me, and when we get a year like this – I keep my flock."

Charles Tulley lived to the astonishing age of 103 years and eleven months, and a newspaper article published on the day following his 101st birthday, gives some measure of the man's vitality and character:

> Mr Charles Tulley, of Hassocks, Sussex, celebrated his 101st birthday yesterday by working in his snow-covered garden. He laughed at the bitter wind and sang as he worked. "I would just as soon see snow as anything else," he said. "Everything in its season and all is full of good use."

To see all the cars parked in the Western Approach nowadays (2000AD) makes it hard to believe that at one time the place was the village green, and served as a venue for fetes, carnivals and travelling fairs. It was even a chosen meeting spot for the Southdown foxhounds, the only concession to the petrol engine being a small garage housed in an old army hut opposite the Clayton Park Hotel.

Opposite: A Kodak carnival float by the wooden hut on the green at Station Approach West. The building contained two businesses: 1. a garage run by a Mr John Cornell and Mr Yule Denman and 2. a photographic studio, run by a Mr de Witt. As a point of interest, the Kodak Girl was a Miss Hemsley and the Kodak Brownie (the little boy in the centre) was Sir Donald Sinden, the actor. His father, maternal grandfather and other relations are also in the group.

Garage
Take a "KODAK"
VELOX

Clayton Park Hotel – looking west

Clayton Park Hotel – looking east. The wagon in the centre of the picture belonged to Hurstpierpoint college and was used to carry the boys' luggage to and from the station.

The old Knifeboard Bus – Mr William Cherriman (driving). Passengers include the Rev. F. G. Finch (Curate of Hurst, 1915-19) and Postman J. Winton. The bus plyed the route for over thirty years, and when it finally came off the road, took part in the Lord Mayor of London's Show.

A charming addition to the scene was a horse-drawn conveyance, which owing to the peculiar disposition of its seats, was known in the coach building trade as a 'Knifeboard Bus'. The service which started around 1890 was founded by a Mr Ellis and ran between Hurstpierpoint and the railway station, the original bus being an open carriage that was drawn by a team of horses.The passengers must have been a hardy lot, for it was only covered over in the winter months.

Nevertheless, the business obviously thrived, as the owner later acquired a two decked motor bus fitted with such luxuries as curtains and foot warmers. Mr Ellis eventually sold the business to Mr William Cherriman (the man whose name is chiefly associated with the enterprise) and he, followed by his son, continued to operate a mixture of motorised and horse drawn transport along the route for many years. Ultimately the horses were phased out, and then in 1936, the company was taken over by Southdown Motor Services.

Stanford Avenue. The porter is taking someone's luggage to the train.

Looking west from the Railway Station

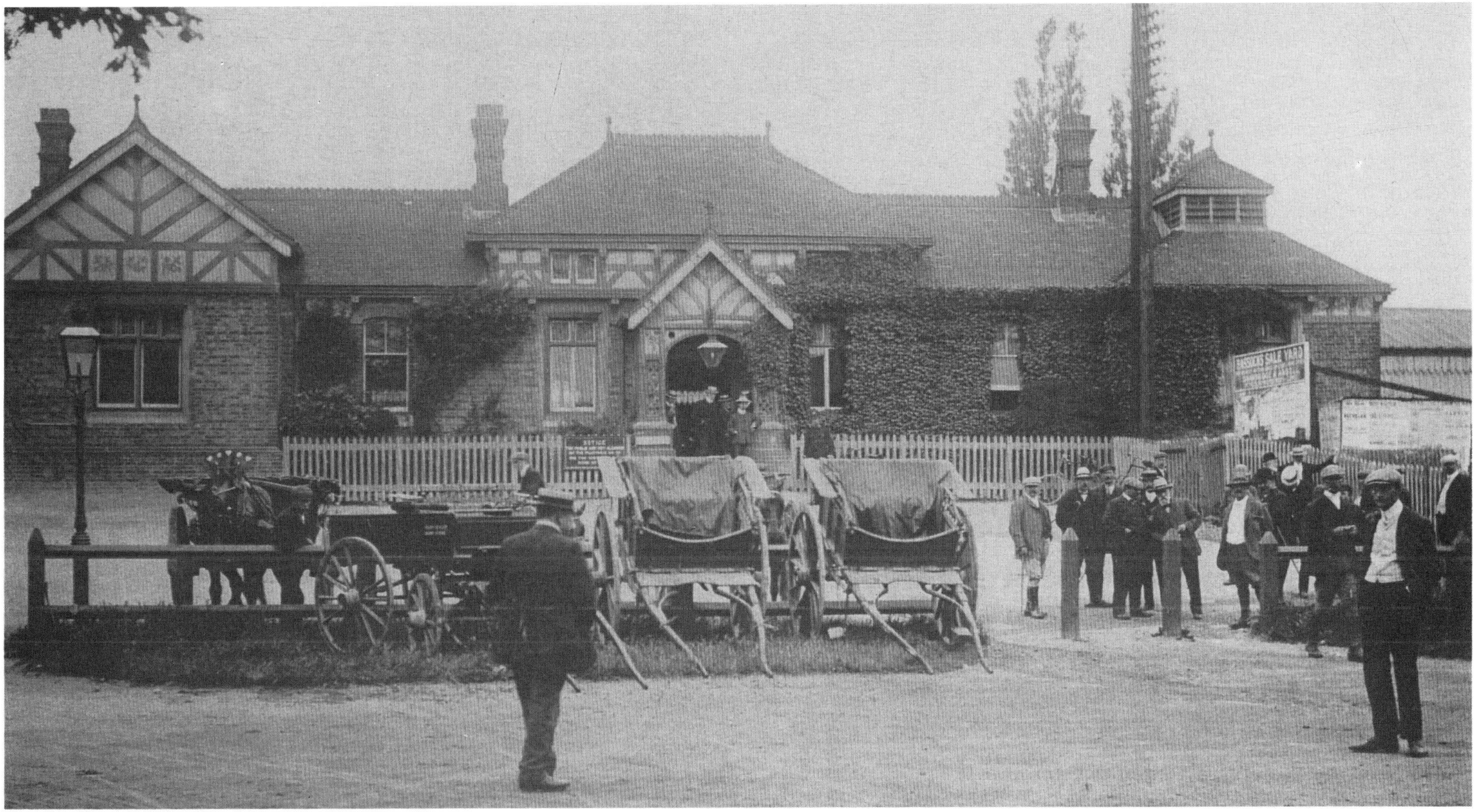

The eastern side of Hassocks station on market day

Describing the eastern side of the station as it was before the First World War, the late Cyril Charman, a life-long resident of Hassocks, and a reliable authority on local history, had this to say:

> There were special milk trains then, and mornings and evenings the approach was full of horse-drawn carts loaded with churns. I can remember perhaps ten or fifteen of them tied to the railings, while the drivers refreshed themselves at the Hassocks Hotel.
>
> The cattle pens were behind the fence between the hotel and the station, and livestock was driven there from far and wide, although calves were sometimes transported in old carts with nets over the top. After school, or at holiday times, children could often earn a penny or two helping to drive the animals back to the farms.
>
> Those were good old days – and I recall Hassocks and Ditchling running a joint carnival that was held annually in the grounds of the Hassocks Hotel. There were roundabouts, boat swings, hoopla, and all the fun of the fair. Many of the sideshows overflowed into the yard at the front of the building, and onto the big lawn between the hotel and the houses in Station Approach. The procession started at Ditchling crossroads, which was a long way to walk for bandsmen and people in fancy dress, so in later years the carnival was held in the field to the west of the Water Company's sub-station along the Ditchling Road.

Before moving on from the station approaches, we would like to return to the subject of horse drawn buses and finishwith an anecdote from a letter by a Mrs Salisbury-Smith (née Stafford), that appeared in an early edition of the *Hassocks and Keymer Talk About.*

> In 1911, two such vehicles operated between Hassocks and Ditchling, and they belonged to a Mr White. In the winter he drove a one-horse black Maria type, with a step at the rear where the conductor stood, while in the summer months, a two horse open topped ex Landau affair was used.

As a girl, Mrs Salisbury-Smith attended school at Burgess Hill, which she went to by train from Hassocks. She often travelled by horse bus to the station, and usually sat on top at the front alongside Mr White. Those trips remained "cherished memories" and she recalled that:

> The glorious climax of the journey came at the entrance to Station Approach. Mr White would hand me the reins just as the horses cantered up the slope, swung round in a wide circle, and pulled up with a flourish in front of the Station steps. I felt sure that they could not have performed the manoeuvre without my assistance, though I did wonder sometimes when I watched them walk off with the empty bus, quite on their own, and park themselves under the oak tree in front of the Station Hotel.

The Station Hotel

Hassocks Wood

One of the great attractions of Hassocks during the early days of the community was a privately owned wood that stretched east from the cinder path to the bank of the Herring Stream. Containing a splendid variety of trees, and interspersed with pretty glades, the place was very dear to the hearts of the local people, who resisting all attempts to exclude them, treated it as common property. So strong was their attachment that repeated representations were made at council level to acquire the land for public recreation, but to no avail. Despite this, the village children continued to play within its boundaries, and make camps in the bracken, and if occasionally turned out by the keeper or a policeman, what did it matter? It gave their fun a spice of adventure. Older youths engaged in rough and tumbles on the springy turf, courting couples loved its seclusion, and people of all ages enjoyed strolling down the leafy pathways. In short, it was so extensively used that it became a sort of district park.

With the outbreak of war in 1914, this was to change for ever. In addition to her young men, Hassocks also gave of her wood. Many a fine tree was converted to trench props and tent pegs, and in consequence, the place was reduced to such a shadow of its former self, that even the rooks, resident there since time immemorial, had to seek accommodation anew. When the war was over, workmen appeared again, and proceeded to cut and chop and hack and saw, until a mere handful of trees remained. The villagers not only witnessed the destruction of their beloved wood, but to add insult to injury, were not told why, although rumours of building intentions were rife. In due course these rumours proved to be correct, the land was divided into plots and a small estate was built on the site. Originally called 'The Firs', it is now known as Clayton Avenue.

The following extract was taken from an article dealing with the vicinity that first appeared in the *Hassocks and Keymer Talkabout*. The author, who was reminiscing about his childhood during the Second World War, said:

> Clayton Avenue was one of my regular haunts, and I recall that almost blocking it west of the footpath to the high street, was a patch of scrubby bushes. Like many other roads in the district, it was unmade, and the sandy surface, cushioned by years of fallen pine needles, contained deep depressions that during wet weather, filled into enormous puddles. Further on towards the railway there was a large Scots pine, and one of its boughs swept so low that it almost brushed your hair. Suspended beneath I had the good luck to discover a goldcrest's nest. Shaped like a pendant, and skilfully constructed with dry grass, leaves and moss, it was superbly camouflaged and despite the proximity to the road, the little birds obviously liked the position, for to the best of my recollection, a pair bred there for several years.
>
> The meadows to the north of Butcher's Wood had not been built on then, and there were uninterrupted views all the way to the Downs. Beyond the goldcrest's tree, the road dipped and swung to the north, and at this point a track continued to the cinderpath. To the left of this track and flowing in a deep gully was a brook, and to the right, a disused sand pit, which at its lowest level had developed into a swamp full of bulrushes and small interconnecting pools. These provided a habitat for amphibians such as frogs and greater crested newts. Rising from the water's edge was a cliff, and on sunny days, lizards, apparently

oblivious to the pull of gravity, scampered over the surface, while further on, sand martins had tunnelled into the rock face, giving it the appearance of a huge worm eaten panel.

At the top of the cliff was a grassy plateau with clumps of bracken and gorse, as well as the occasional pine tree or silver birch. It was a good place to see glow worms, after dark, and on one side the ground sloped down to the previously mentioned track.

It was on this slope that I taught a friend to ride, although that is probably overstating the case, for in fact all I actually did was to promise him that I wouldn't let go. Armed with this assurance, he trustingly mounted my little green bicycle, and I – without the slightest twinge of conscience – gave it a hearty shove.

The sand pit also served as a battleground for opposing groups of village boys, and the weapon they used was called a pug stick. This was a 'whippy' hazel rod about four feet in length, with a clod of mud (pug) moulded around the head. The combatant would flick the stick, causing the pug to fly off at great speed. With practice it could be pitched with alarming accuracy, which meant that the participants got pretty filthy. But it was great fun, until that is, the more unruly elements rather spoiled things by taking potshots at passers-by. Inevitably word reached the ear of the police, and to give an indication of how times have changed, all it took to disperse the mobs of youngsters, was the sight of the local bobby, with cape neatly folded over the handlebars of his bicycle, riding purposefully up the avenue.

The goldcrests have long departed, as has their tree, and most of the other little creatures that made the area their home. The wild lads are respectable grandparents now, and their former playground is just a memory – a lovely memory to be sure – but no more than that. Such a desirable site could hardly escape the developers, and by the time they were through, the last vestige of the old wood disappeared.

Hassocks Wood

Looking south from Chancellors Park – since this photograph was taken the building housing Woodsland stores has been extended to twice the size.

Spitalford Bridge, Hassocks School and the Herring Stream

The road through Hassocks descends gently to Spitalford Bridge, the name Spitalford also being that of a former farmhouse in the area. The origin of 'spital' is uncertain, and what follows is mere supposition on our part. It is possible that it derives from the German, where the word means 'infirmary' or hospital, and if that is the case, there might well have been some sort of poor man's shelter at this point. There is a Spital Road in Lewes (close to the prison) where two ancient highways cross, and we understand that in the eleventh century, this was where the founder of Lewes Priory built and endowed the Spital of St. Nicholas, to dispense relief and hospitality to pilgrims and travellers. Unfortunately however, as far as Hassocks is concerned, the old farmhouse, which might have provided clues of a previous use, was demolished in 1875, and to date, no further evidence has been forthcoming.

The Clayton and Keymer South District School was erected on the farm site, and the building remains there to this day. It is adjacent to the thoroughfare but stands at a lower level, and steps lead down to the playground. A shop on the corner opposite is also in a noticeably lower position. We are not at all sure why this should be, but the late Cyril Charman thought he knew the answer. The reason, he suggested, was that both the highway and the land on its southern side, stretching east from the junction of Downsview Road to the stream, had been artificially raised with spoil removed from the cutting beneath the railway line.

> That would have accounted for the low school playground and the much higher land where the garage now stands. It was certainly built on made-up ground. Compare the high bank of the stream on its western side with the low back gardens of the Parklands Road houses. When I was a boy, the difference was even more more apparent.

In addition to its function as a seat of learning, the new premises also served as a meeting place for the Keymer Parish Council. And on one such occasion (described in the *Mid Sussex Times* as a 'Matchlight Gathering') the elected worthies, after assembling for their discussions, discovered they were unable to get in, as workmen engaged in renovating the premises, had failed to return the key.

> A search led to nothing, and so the business was transacted in the open air, outside the building. The chairman found seating accommodation on a trestle, his colleagues stood around him smoking their pipes. However, it soon grew dark, and as it was a moonless night, matches were brought into use. Protected from the wind by hats, and despite the difficulties of the situation and the scorching of fingers, the meeting was duly carried through.
>
> No one seemed desirous of suggesting "any other business" and in the darkness the clerk packed up his books and the faithful separated – not forgetting to close the gates of the forecourt. What added to the humour of the situation was the fact that a substantial sum of money was being voted for public lighting, when those who were doing so had extreme trouble in obtaining sufficient light for themselves.

Hassocks School

To return to Spitalford Bridge, this was originally built by public subscription in 1817, and rebuilt sixty years later when Mr William Wood was Surveyor for Clayton, and Mr Joseph Hammond was the Surveyor for Keymer. It spans the Herring[1] Stream, which rising from the Downs at Clayton, runs north across the meadows, skirts the eastern extremities of Laggs Wood and Butchers' Wood, passes through the village, then veers west to the railway embankment where a spacious tunnel enables it to flow unimpeded to the far side. This stream, once commercially important to the district, is a main tributary of the Adur, and joins the river near Shermanbury. In the past it operated waterwheels at Hammonds Mill, Ruckford Mill and Cobbs Mill, the sites of which still reveal traces of former use.

Looking down from Spitalford Bridge gives one little idea of the potential for destruction that lurks in the babbling brook below. Yet after periods of prolonged rainfall, it has been known to rise dramatically, burst its banks and flood the highway to a considerable depth. Traffic has been halted, and pedestrians wishing to keep their feet dry have been ferried along the Keymer Road in small, shallow draughted boats.

Incidents so described have occurred in living memory, at a time when water levels have never been as low. Therefore it is interesting to reflect that in the distant past, when the Weald was covered by the forest of Andreswald and harboured wolves and wild boars, water levels were between sixty and a hundred feet higher than they are now. Dry watercourses today were brooks then, and brooks today were once rivers.

[1]Herring is a Saxon word denoting a shoaling or meeting place

Precisely what the area would have looked like we can only guess, but excavations at Friars Oak Farm during the construction of the golf course have revealed traces of an ancient fishing community, which makes it reasonable to suppose that much of the land to the north and west of Hassocks was flooded. If that was the case, then the major source of water would have undoubtedly have been the Herring Stream.

Dale House and the Hassocks Cinema

> I was always curious about the old ruin that stood alongside the Studio Cinema at Hassocks. Not that there was much to see, encroaching brambles and ivy had blurred the outline of the remaining brickwork, while moss and stinging nettles all but concealed the surviving traces of some delicate mosaic flooring.The near total destruction made it impossible to estimate how large the structure had been although the shattered remains of some ornate terra cotta urns, and the paved surround of a former goldfish pond, suggested that it had been a dwelling of some quality.
>
> (Extract from 'The Old Century' by Mark Dudeney.)

In days gone by, the road to Keymer was lined with many large and splendid properties, all occupied by wealthy families and their servants. One such place was Dale House, a huge rambling premises that stood on the site of the present junction with Dale Avenue. The late George Cragg, a great authority on the area, had vivid recollections of this particular building, and of those who resided within:

> It possessed a long frontage and stretched to what is now the eastern side of Orion Parade, where there was a sizeable billiards room. During the early 1920s. the house was the home of the Haig family.

Village celebration at the ending of the First World War. The large house to the right of the picture was Holmwood, the home of the Shand family, who were great benefactors to the district.

Looking east along Keymer Road. Dale House is partly concealed by trees.

Rear view of Dale House

General Haig lived there with his young wife and two sisters. He was a retired Indian Army officer and a cousin to the better known Earl Haig, the former First World War Field Marshal. Also resident was the General's batman, Charlie Burgess, and his wife who acted as housekeeper. In addition there was Mr Tomy, the gardener, Monty, the groom, and Pincher, a lurcher dog that followed the horses whenever they were exercised.

The southern aspect was extremely pleasant. Large bay windows looked over an immaculate gravel drive to trim lawns and well tended flower beds and rockeries. A stream which contained clumps of king-cups and was spanned by a rustic bridge, meandered through the grounds, and beyond that, a lake stocked with giant carp, and with two islands, provided a perfect habitat for swans and ducks. The gardener's bungalow, two rows of stables and a coach house, with a cobbled yard between, stood where numbers 2, 4 and 6 Dale Avenue stand now, and further south still, there was a large greenhouse and the kitchen garden. My father was employed to carry out maintenance work at the property, and I sometimes lent a hand. On one occasion I pushed our builder's handcart with four five-gallon drums all the way from Dale House to Ditchling, where I went to Mr Slater's slaughterhouse in East Gardens. He filled up the drums with animal's blood, then I pushed them back again. The smell was horrid, but Mr Tomy said it was a wonderful fertiliser and poured it round the grapevines.

General Haig was a real gentleman, and very friendly with Mr Goreham, the squire of Telscombe. Once a year the children of that village came to Dale House, and a sports-day and 'bun fight' were held within the grounds.

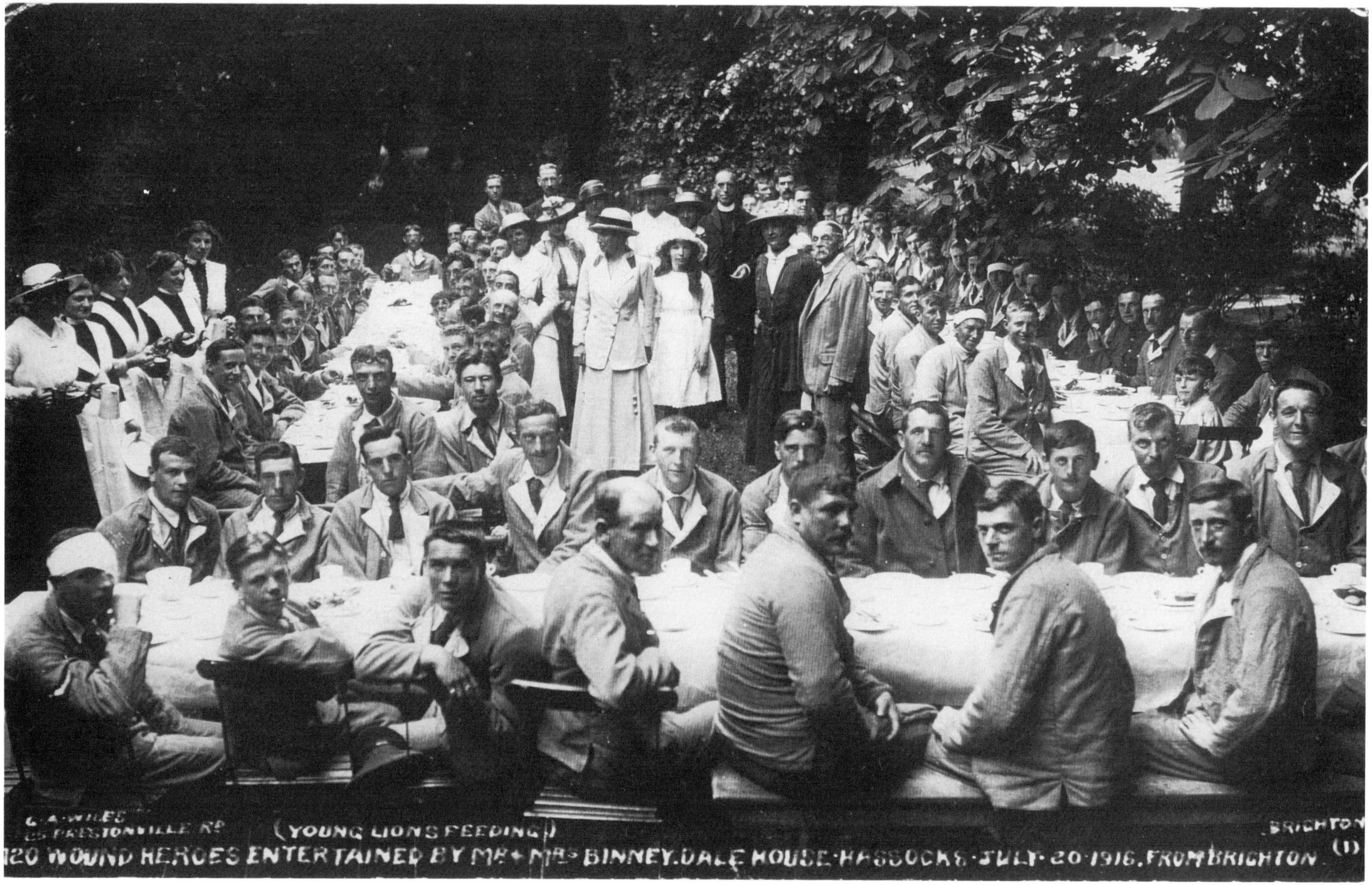

Wounded soldiers being entertained at Dale House, Mr and Mrs Binney are standing centre right.

Prior to the Haig's occupancy, a Mr and Mrs Binney resided at Dale House, and judging by available information, would appear to have been a particularly warm-hearted and generous couple. They lived there during the First World War, and like many other people, did all they could to support the morale of British fighting men. Soldiers on leave in Hassocks were always encouraged to pay them a visit, and an indication of the kindness and hospitality they invariably received, was alluded to many years later in a brief letter from a lady to the *Hassocks and Keymer Talkabout:*

> "I was in service at Dale House in 1919, " she wrote, "and it was there that I met and courted my husband. He was one of the many soldiers made welcome by the Binney's. They gave him refreshments, cigarettes, and of all things – socks!"

Invitations to Dale House were extended far beyond the boundaries of Hassocks, all were made welcome, and the more that came the merrier. Open-topped charabancs, loaded with wounded soldiers from hospitals in Brighton would be driven up from the coast, and the veterans treated to a day of unstinting entertainment.

It was not just the Binney's who displayed gratitude to the nation's heroes, people from the village also expressed their appreciation, and the way that they did it was by congregating near Spitalford Bridge, then, as the vehicles conveying these brave men set off for the homeward journey, a cheering crowd showered them with sweets and cigarettes.

Before the Binney's moved to the district, a Mr and Mrs Hamilton lived at Dale House. Their son Patrick was born at that address and in later life became a novelist of some distinction. At the height of his popularity, he was regarded by many as being a latter day Charles Dickens, a view that seems barely credible now, although at least two of his works, 'Rope' and 'Gaslight', are still well known. Yet despite the advantage of background and early literary success, Patrick Hamilton appears to have led a dissolute type of existence. In gathering material for his novels and plays, he spent a great deal of time 'soaking up' the atmosphere and low life in countless back street public houses. It led to alcoholism, and at a comparatively early age, this gifted but flawed man drank himself to death.

For reasons that are a mystery to us, Dale House was knocked down in the 1930s, and in due course the site was acquired by a business concern known as the 'Fletcher-Barnett syndicate'. They built a cinema on the land, it was named the Studio, and from start to finish the project took only fifteen weeks to complete, and that included diverting the course of the kingcup stream, a job that had to be done before the foundations could be laid. The builders and most of the sub-contractors were from the neighbouring area, and nearly all the men employed were local workers. Everything for the comfort of the patrons had been attended to. Seats were of the sloping back type, an air-purifying plant was installed, the acoustics were excellent, and the interior was tastefully decorated in cream, green and pink. Major Kenneth Johnston was appointed the first manager. The opening ceremony was performed by Sir William Campion on November 28th, 1938, and on the previous evening the proprietors entertained a number of honoured guests and VIPs to a celebration dinner at the Downs Hotel. After the meal and speeches, the company adjourned to the cinema for a private viewing of the first film – 'The Prisoner of Zenda', starring Ronald Coleman and Madeleine Carroll. This film, with a full supporting programme, was shown for three days and followed for the remainder of the week by Jon Hall, Dorothy Lamour, Raymond Massey and C. Aubrey Smith in 'The Hurricane.'

There were continuous performances from 2pm to 10.30pm on weekdays and Saturdays. 7.30pm to 10pm on Sundays. Prices of admission to adults ranged from sixpence (2.5p) to one shilling and sixpence (7.5p), with concessions for children. The best and therefore the most expensive seats were in the balcony, and all were bookable in advance.

This village cinema was often referred to as the 'West End' in the country, and there was more than a grain of truth in the assertion, for it was a luxurious, near-glamorous building and compared favourably with the great picture palaces at Brighton. In its hey day during the mid to late 1940s, queues for Saturday evening performances often extended all the way to Parkmore Terrace. At

Souvenir programme of the Studio Cinema at its opening in 1938

the time a new manager, Mr Ridley, was in charge, and as the patrons entered the foyer, he would be there, impeccably attired in evening dress and offering them a cordial welcome. He thoroughly enjoyed the spotlight and frequently appeared on the stage himself to inform the audience of the pleasures to come, not that it was strictly necessary, for future entertainment was well advertised. The advance publicity for 'King Kong' being a case in point, hoardings at Hassocks railway station were plastered with posters depicting the giant ape and the impact they created amongst the local lads was enormous. Although an old film, it was immensely popular and despite the censor's refusal to grant a U certificate (thus allowing children to see a film without being accompanied by an adult), every youngster in the district was determined to get in. That they succeeded is beyond dispute, for the show was a complete sell-out, and those who arrived late were unable to get seats for love or money.

During the post-war period, there was a change of ownership, and the Studio was renamed the Orion. It prospered for a while, and then, like many similar establishments, had to face up to the challenge of television. It was a battle in the short term that could never be won, despite the introduction of cinemascope, three dimensional pictures, and a host of other gimmicks, and the numbers visiting the place dwindled to the point where the end seemed inevitable.

In 1963, on the twenty-fifth anniversary of its opening, there was a celebration and a repeat of the original programme. The manager confidently assured those present that the future was bright. "We now look forward to the next twenty-five years," he said. But they were empty words. The following year the Orion closed pending demolition. And when workmen started to pull it down, the last, and not entirely dry-eyed audience was outside the cinema, not in.

It is of interest to note that C. Aubrey Smith, who appeared in the 'Hurricane" was a great sportsman, and brought cricket to Hollywood. He also had local connections, insofar that during his earlier years he played football for Burgess Hill.

Wilmington Lodge, the Adastra Park and the Stafford family

Beyond Orion Parade, a high wooden fence on the northern side of the road, borders the grounds of Wilmington Lodge. The original property has gone, but it warrants remembrance if only because Mr Manning, a former occupant, reputedly papered the walls of the study with worthless share certificates that he had purchased throughout his life.

Keymer Road, looking west towards Hassocks

The Adastra Park

East of Wilmington Lodge lies Adastra Park, an area of land that was presented to the community by one of its greatest benefactors, Mr Edward Stafford, the wealthy owner of Villa Adastra, which was formerly known as Wentworth House. Mr Stafford, according to an old directory, ran a fancy bazaar in Brighton's Western Road, and it would appear to have been a profitable enterprise, for his home was very much on the grand scale, being what used to be described as a 'carriage' house. The carriage driveway came out where the main entrance to the park now is.

The name Adastra was taken from the motto of the Royal Air Force, Per Ardua Ad Astra *(Way to the stars)*

The Staffords had two sons and two daughters, and in 1916, during the First World War, their eldest, a lad named Ewart, enlisted in the Royal Flying Corps straight from school. On completing his training, he was despatched to the Front where almost immediately he took part in a series of flying missions over German held territory. What happened next is contained in a first hand account that was published in the *Hassocks and Keymer Talk About.* The writer, a former R. F. C Officer, Mr A. B. Fanstone, stated:

> He [Stafford] was shot down at Arras while on dawn patrol on 9th April, 1917 during the Arras 'push'. Although badly wounded, he skilfully managed to crash land just inside our lines (on ground taken from the enemy only a few hours previously). His Observer unwounded, clambered out into a shell hole and survived. Ewart was eventually rescued very weak from loss of blood. Gangrene set in, a leg was amputated but he died a few days later in the base hospital at Abbeville. I am able to give these details as I was in the same engagement and saw Ewart just before his last flight, and afterwards in the field hospital.

Stafford's parents received permission from the War Office to visit their boy, and were at his bedside during his final hours. Ewart died on Sunday April 22nd, 1917 and was buried at the soldier's cemetery, Abbeville.

In 1999, the *Mid Sussex Times* published a weekly series entitled 'The History of Mid Sussex in the 20th Century' and under a subheading 'A fitting memorial to the lads that died', they made reference to Ewart Stafford's death and its effect on the district:

> After the war, Mr Stafford began to draw up plans for a Garden of Remembrance to his son and other fallen heroes from Keymer and Hassocks. He chose a strip of land fronting Keymer Road that had once formed part of the garden to his villa. Mr J. Charlton from Tunbridge Wells was selected as the designer and the garden opened to the public in 1924. No expense was spared. A finely carved lych gate was reflected in a shallow pond by the western entrance and a central path through the garden led to an Italian pergola covered with roses and wisteria. In the centre of the pergola, was a bird bath with a bronze figure, whose hand held a bird poised for flight. Carved round the rim of the bird bath were the words: "The bird of life is on the wing" and "Ewart Stafford, Abbeville, 1917". Further along the path was a sundial, bearing the message, "After darkness, light." The pathway ended with a large wooden shelter containing seats. The names of the fallen were carved in the timber, with the inscription, "When peace returns to the countryside, our thanks shall be to the lads who died."

The Bird of Life

Lydia Lidstone described the garden in an article published in the *Sussex County Magazine*, in 1924.

> It is difficult to convey in words the spirit of peace and beauty that haunts this Garden of Memory. Sometimes on quiet summer evenings when the fragrance of the roses fills the air, one sees little groups of people resting there after the heat and toil of the day. Some of those whose husbands and sons will never return to them. As they sit there and gaze at the distant Downs, all aglow in the fire of the sunset, their eyes seem to look beyond, until they see among the poppyfields, 'That little bit of France whose name shall be forever England.'

The commemorative oak

On April 22nd, 1926 (the ninth anniversary of Ewart's death) an oak sapling commemorating his father's gifts of park and garden to the inhabitants of the parish, was ceremoniously planted in the grounds by Mrs Stafford – and it grows there still.

Just over two years later, on October 31st, 1928, in an act of unprecedented generosity, Edward Stafford bequeathed the Villa Adastra, together with three and a half acres of lovely gardens to the Salvation Army, and the organisation converted it into an Eventide Home for the elderly. To compound the gesture, he later donated £1000 towards the construction of a new wing for the property. In the meantime, he and his wife moved to Thatchets, which was a considerably smaller residence on the other side of the road and he lived there for the rest of his life. This great-hearted man died in 1947, and in accordance with his dearest wish, his ashes were scattered in the Garden of Remembrance, the memorial created for his eldest son.

A well-known verse inscribed on one of the seats within, reads:

> The kiss of the sun for pardon,
> The song of the birds for mirth,
> One is nearer God's heart in a garden
> Than anywhere else on earth.

It is a sentiment that was sweetly and sincerely expressed, but much has changed since then. The garden remains, and is still pleasant to visit, while plaques to the memory of the Staffords ensure that their association with the place will never be forgotten. However, the views of the Downs are concealed by houses. The pool lies buried beneath a car park. The sundial and the bird of life have vanished. The shelter has been dismantled. Even the lych gates have been lifted from their hinges and removed, who knows where? And the peace and tranquillity so eloquently described by Lydia Lidstone has gone forever. It is the fumes of petrol, not the scent of roses that now fills the air, and any birdsong is muffled by the noise of passing traffic.

The Box Brothers of Parkside

During the 1930s, two brothers by the names of Gordon and Cecil Box, purchased a field to the north of Villa Adastra. Gordon, who was the younger, was the Principal of a commercial college in St. George's Place (near St. Peter's Church) in Brighton, and there he taught book keeping, Pitman's shorthand and typing. One of his students, the late Ursula Rice of Hassocks recalled:

> Mr Box and his brother were always full of good works. On Sundays they would give gramophone recitals at local hospitals.

A beneficiary of their charitable actions was a Mr Brock, who knew the brothers when he was an orphan boy. His firm recollection was that they were devout Christian philanthropists, who spent their money on trying to brighten the lives of children made homeless by the war. His view was confirmed in part by a Mr Rogers of Brighton. He was a former acquaintance of the Box's, and in a letter published by the *Hassocks and Keymer Talkabout* he described their background and the reason for acquiring the land.

> As I knew them very well and shared in their activities, I thought it would be of interest to relate a little of the story of these two remarkable men.
>
> Throughout their adult lives, Gordon and Cecil Box devoted the whole of their spare time to visiting hospitals, infirmaries and orphanages, bringing all sorts of cheer to those within. Gordon's main interest was in the welfare of children, and Cecil looked after the needs of the adults. One of their activities was running an annual camp for boys, most of whom came from orphanages. I went myself in about 1924, and we camped at Danny barn near Wolstonbury. After a few years, the venue was changed to Albourne, and then, in the early 1930s, the brothers decided to buy some ground at the rear of Villa Adastra, the idea being to establish a permanent site there. I went along to see it and recall a large area of grassland, a small wood, and a stream at the northern end, while on the western side, iron railings separated it from the park. Probably because of its close vicinity, they called the place Parkside and quickly developed it into a camping ground. A hut was built that would provide sleeping accommodation for up to fifty, tables and seats were installed round it, more trees were planted (including a grove of silver birches) and a slide together with a plank swing, ordinary swings, a see-saw and a roundabout were erected for the children, finally, the stream was dammed and widened to form a pool. The site was not only used for the annual camp, it was also available for schools, Sunday schools and any other youth organisation that expressed an interest in using it. Gordon and Cecil did most of the work and Cecil was the cook.

Mr Brock, who was mentioned earlier, also submitted some

memoirs of childhood and of the outings that he made to Parkside. These too were published in the *Hassocks and Keymer Talkabout*, and what follows is an extract.

> I was put in the Children's Home at Shoreham (a former workhouse) in 1947, and stayed there until 1953. Either Mr Gordon or Mr Cecil Box used to visit it once a week to take us for gymnastics or games. In the summer we camped for a fortnight in their beautiful grounds at Hassocks, the younger boys using a large verandahed hut as dormitory, while the older boys slept under canvas. I also remember a stream and a luminous silver birch grove where religious services were held. There was a wood where we played hide and seek and cowboys and Indians, and I will never forget the slide, down which – to the astonishment of the brothers – slid Mrs Box, who was well in her eighties!

In a similar vein, a lady visitor recalled:

> When our Brighton school had their annual visit to Parkside, it was a very enjoyable afternoon for children and teachers alike, and after the youngsters had tired of the pool, Mr Gordon Box played 'Bears in the Wood' with them. The brothers took great pride in their grounds and worked hard to maintain them.

Gordon and Cecil Box have been dead for many years now, they slipped away almost unnoticed. Parkside too has gone, buried beneath concrete, and the only witnesses to its existence are the children who once went there. They would be parents and grandparents themselves now, and probably for most, the happy holidays spent at Hassocks and the kindly benefactors who made them possible, are either forgotten or remain just warm but hazy memories.

Campaigners Sports Day (approx 1958/59) with Clans from Brighton, Haywards Heath and Hurstpierpoint Evangelical Free Churches. The gentleman in the light coloured suit, seated in the centre left background is one of the Mr Box's, while addressing the youngsters is the Vicar of Bishop Hannington Church, Hove.

The Villa Adastra

Stafford House

Keymer

Stafford House and the Downs Hotel ~ St. Anne's School for Girls and Merton House, Down Under, Lodge Lane and the Dusty Road ~ The King of Keymer ~ The Grey Lady ~ The Greyhound and Keymer Church ~ Uncle Mac and Oldlands

From Villa Adastra to the village of Keymer is but a step, the road curves uphill and at its highest point may be seen yet another fine Victorian property known as Stafford House. Originally called Bloomfields, it was once the home of a Mr Munster, who owned a lot of property in the area, including the old manor house, and the site on the corner of Lodge Lane, where the Catholic Church now stands. Local resident George Cragg recalled:

> At one time some Canadian soldiers were billeted on the land, and the hut they built for their accommodation was later used as a Catholic Church. But it was only a temporary affair and in due course was knocked down and replaced by a more permanent building.

However, to return to Bloomfields. This was eventually purchased by the man whose name has appeared so often in these pages, Mr Edward Stafford. Readers will recall that he donated Villa Adastra to the elderly. Bloomfields he gave to the young, presenting it to the East Sussex County Council upon trust, to be used for educational purposes in the interest of service of youth. The grateful authority renamed it Stafford House in his honour, and despite problems that have risen from time to time, a supportive community and a vigilant society known as the Friends of Stafford House, have ensured that it continues to be run in accordance with the donor's wishes. Opposite Stafford House there is a residential area known as Stafford Way. At one time a property called the Downs Hotel stood on the site. Built in 1892, it was a splendid looking establishment and a successful enterprise for many years. Information published in a 1930s Railway Tourist Guide describes its attractions:

> The Hotel that is different:
>
> Seven acres of delightful grounds. One hour from London, 12 minutes from Brighton, Historical locality. Close to Golf Course and facilities for riding. Forty bedrooms, central heating, hot and cold water, Vi-spring mattresses, bedside lights and radiators in every room. Inclusive terms from 15 shillings and sixpence (77½p per day.).

Standing within the grounds was an additional attraction, a sort of health farm known as the Sunnyside Restorium. Containing a resident physician and qualified staff, it was fully equipped with apparatus for the treatment of obesity, rheumatic conditions, debility, massage etc.

Guests came from all walks of life. The names of lords and ladies, government politicians, leading actors and actresses, and well known business tycoons, all adorned the hotel register, and their wishes and wants were effectively dealt with by a staff well used to the vagaries of human nature. However, even they, with all their professional expertise could hardly have been prepared to deal with the inmates of Brighton Workhouse who, during the First World War, were evicted so that the building could be used as a hospital for wounded servicemen. One wonders what the poor folk made of it all. To be moved from their draughty hill top home in East Brighton to the comfort of a luxurious country hotel in genteel Keymer must have been an almost unbelievable experience. It was certainly unbelievable to the local people, who although kind-hearted and generous in many ways, were unable to work up much enthusiasm for the arrangement, and probably heaved a collective sigh of relief when the unexpected visitors eventually departed.

As we have said, guests came from all walks of life, and two at least were destined to achieve international notoriety, according to local resident F. Martin:

My paternal grandfather had a boot shop where we live now, (Keymer Village). He used to make the boots and shoes. I don't know if you know about Dr Crippen who murdered his wife, well, he stayed at the Downs Hotel for a while. My grandfather made a pair of shoes for his secretary, Miss La Neve.

The Downs Hotel

St Anne's School for Girls and Merton House, Down Under, Lodge Lane and the Dusty Road

To the east of the Downs Hotel, a large square-shaped villa, had at some time between the two world wars, been converted to a girl's school called St Anne's. The pupils wore a wine-coloured uniform and were a familiar sight in the area. Richard Wyndam, in his book *South Eastern Survey* (published by Batsford in 1940) includes a photograph of some of the girls and their teachers strolling in a westerly direction along New Way Lane. The caption, with a degree of poetic licence, states, "The Way to School". If that were really so, it would have been a long way indeed, as their school lay in the opposite direction!

Another Keymer school, and one that is still recalled with a great deal of affection, was Merton House, where the children wore green coloured uniform with yellow edging. Founded in the early 1940s by Miss E. R. Thorpe and Miss M. Warburton, two ladies who came down from London in 1939, it commenced operations in the Guide Hut known as Down Under, which stood (and indeed still stands) near the foot of the Downs besides Lodge Lane. The venture was so successful that in a short time they had to look for larger premises and in due course moved to a house called Glenham in Lodge Lane. As it transpired, it was a mere holding exercise, for the school's popularity increased to such a degree, that it became necessary to move yet again, this time to a pair of large semi-detached dwellings in Keymer Road. They have long since vanished, and there is some dispute over precisely which houses they were. George Cragg had no such doubts.

> "They were Melrose and Rushford, and Rose Villa and Waring," he declared. "Waring, which was the easternmost property , was originally called Ditchling Villa, and the school playing fields were on the opposite side of the road."

Tracing the history of Down Under hut has proved to be surprisingly difficult. The earliest written reference that we could find appeared in *Mid Sussex through the Ages,* where it briefly stated:

> The hut was given the name of "Down Under" partly because this was the name given to their homeland by Australian soldiers during the Great War, and partly because it is under the South Downs.

The author, A. H. Gregory, usually a most meticulous writer, was, on this occasion, rather obtuse, and left a lot unsaid. We take him to have meant that the hut was once occupied by Australian troops, although he produces no evidence to support this, but if that was indeed the case, it would have presumably been erected at some time between 1914 and 1918.

What we do know is, the land on which it stands, once belonged to the Danny Estate, and around 1920, was purchased from the Campion family by a Mr and Mrs Hett of Ardingly. They either converted the place (if it was already in situ) or built it themselves as a holiday home.

The Girl Guides involvement began in 1926, when the Hett's whose daughter was the Divisional Commissioner for Mid Sussex, presented it to the movement as a Guideing Centre and a permanent camping site, and for many years afterwards it was used in that capacity.

Then, following the outbreak of the Second World War, the building was sold to Merton House School. We mentioned earlier that this establishment soon found it necessary to move to larger quarters, and so the hut was sold again, the next purchaser being Mrs Turner of nearby Lodge Farm. She re-converted it into holiday accommodation, and then a few years later it was leased by Mr George Watson, a local builder.

The hut remains, but looks sad and dilapidated now, and gives little clue to its former use. The average passer by would scarcely accord it a glance, although they might vaguely wonder about the meaning of the sign which is still fitted above the door.

A Merton House School photograph

Down Under Hut

Just a stone's throw away is Lodge Farm Cottage and former occupiers of the dwelling, Mr and Mrs Sayers, were the subject of an article entitled, 'Days Gone By' that was published in the *Mid Sussex Times* in 1928 – part of which we reproduce here:

> Christmas Day, 1927 had a double significance for Mr and Mrs Reuben Sayers of Lodge Farm Cottage, Keymer. They had spent fifty years at the address and it was also the occasion of their Golden Wedding. Both being natives of Hurstpierpoint, Mrs Sayers, neé Parsons, remembers the funeral of Sir William Campion's grandfather. "It took place on a day when icicles hung off the hedges and buildings." Mr Sayers, who started work as a farmer's boy, recalled the times when he used to go with the carter and a team of horses to Brighton and back. They used to load the wagon with shingle at the spot where the West Pier now stands, and pay for it at a round-house office on the beach. There were no houses on the north side of the (London Road) railway viaduct in those days, and nothing but market gardens opposite Cheapside.
>
> When Mr and Mrs Sayers were first married, Archdeacon Garbett was the Rector of Clayton and Keymer and there were toll gates at the top of Ockley Lane,and near Lodge Farm. The gate near the farm was kept by an old man named Joe Waller. It was only done away with in 1887. Grass used to be scythed for hay, and corn was cut with swap-hooks. Mr Sayers used to cut the corn and his wife would tie it in bundles. Both are contemptuous of the modern reaper-binder, asserting that in these days, farmers waste as much grain as their predecessors used to grow.

In a previous publication (*Edwin Street and the Victoria Pleasure Gardens*) we made mention of the ancient Sheep and Lamb Fair held annually at St. John's Common, now known as Burgess Hill. In order to get to the venue, shepherds and their flocks after travelling many miles over the South Downs, would descend to the Weald at a point near the junction of Lodge Lane and Underhill Lane. Once down, they headed towards Keymer, and continued on to St. John's Common via Ockley Lane. Old residents who have long since passed away, described how, during the early hours of the morning, flock after flock would be driven through the village. The road and pathways were completely blocked with sheep, they said, and remained blocked for a long time. It was utter pandemonium, with ewes bleating, men shouting and dogs barking. Then, after they had gone, everything was smothered with a thick layer of dust. With regard to this, it is perhaps not widely realised that in Mid Sussex, tarmacadamed road surfaces have only been with us for a hundred years or so, hence all of the dust. In the old days it was necessary to water the highway at regular intervals during long hot spells, otherwise conditions became intolerable. Keymer had a good record in this respect, but not so neighbouring Ditchling, as may be gathered from an article comparing the two districts that was published in the *Mid Sussex Times* in 1907.

> There is no proper road watering (in Ditchling) and the affairs were so bad on Friday, when the wind was high and the dust almost choking individuals, that the householders were seen watering the roads from pails.

A group in Lodge Lane – from left to right: Mr Waller, a rug maker, Canon Malaby, a retired churchman who lived in Keymer Road, Mr Collinson, who worked for the local coal merchants, and Jesse Hillman who had a dairy next to the village post office. The motorcycle, a Douglas, belonged to Gilbert Stephenson, who in later years was the PT Instructor at Merton House School.

> Could not some better arrangements than this be made for road watering here? No doubt the County Council would bear part of the expense. A parishioner informs us that the provision of a water cart for Ditchling was talked about in connection with Queen Victoria's Diamond Jubilee – ten years ago, but the idea gave place to another scheme. Ditchling has many charms in the summer. But, oh, the dust! A person walking from Hassocks railway station into Ditchling cannot fail to note the contrast. On the east side of the station and through Keymer the roads are nicely watered, and the trees and gardens and everything looks fresh and beautiful, but almost immediately on leaving Keymer village – unless it is just after a heavy downpour of rain – one finds the hedges white with dust, one begins to breathe "thick air",and reaching Ditchling, sees, if one's eyes are not absolutely smothered, roads being practically blown away by degrees!

The Keymer water cart was garaged at Mr Cragg's farm in Lodge Lane, and as a point of interest, this same farmer also provided a cart for the area's refuse collection service, and found his own tip!

The King of Keymer, the Grey Lady, the Greyhound and Keymer Church

> 'The chief glory of Keymer Village in the summer', it was recorded in 1883, 'is the annual flower show – a splendid development of a well managed Horticultural Society – and it is held in August and patronised by many of the elite and fashionables of Brighton, the event being quite a gala day in the parish.
>
> (Extract from *Mid-Sussex through the Ages*)

The founder and promoter of this flower show, described in the *Mid Sussex Times* as ranking second only to Brighton for its beauty, was a Mr Hugh Saunders of Eastfield Lodge. A great benefactor to the district, and an immensely popular man, he was affectionately known as the King of Keymer, and was regarded as its guide, philosopher and friend. Mr Saunders had been a wine and spirits merchant in Brighton for many years and was a lessee of the Blacksmith Arms in North Street. It was his success in business that enabled him to purchase the land on which he built his home, a property that, according to George Cragg, 'was a beautiful country residence. Having a surprisingly shy disposition for a man of his background, he was quite content to take a back seat and upon retirement, steadfastly refused the municipal offers that were his for the taking. He preferred instead to lead the life of a country gentleman, and to keep an open house for the many friends and acquaintances who visited him. In this respect he was generosity itself and the hospitality afforded to his guests was truly proverbial.

Hugh Saunders died in 1881, and no royal personage could have been more sincerely mourned. Over 250 people from the south coast alone attended his funeral, a special train being laid on to transport them to Hassocks. And to give further indication of the esteem in which he was held, nearly all of the shops in Brighton closed for the day.

Ghost stories are not our normal stock in trade, we prefer to deal with realities, which are far more interesting. However, there are exceptions to every rule, and when the source of the information is Cyril Charman, then it is surely worth recording:

> In 1922, when I worked in Keymer, there was much talk of the Grey Lady, a ghostly figure supposedly seen by many people in the village. I never saw her myself, but she was said to be tall, stately, and always in grey. Sometimes she was observed in the road near the old manor house, and on other occasions, walking up the churchyard path and entering the church itself. My employer, a man who had both feet firmly on the ground, was convinced of her existence, and because there were so many reported sightings, I became rather interested and mentioned the matter to the Rector.

Keymer: showing former district school

> A short time later, he drew me to one side and said quite seriously, "I think I have seen your Grey Lady, Cyril." He then told me that during Evensong the previous day, he had opened his eyes momentarily, and saw a lady dressed in grey in one of the side pews. She was a stranger to him, so upon finishing he went to speak to her – but it was not to be. There was no lady, the pew was empty. To add to the mystery, not a single member of the congregation had noticed her, and the Usher was adamant that no one had left the building. The Rector it would seem was the only witness to her presence, and he, poor man, probably wished that he had kept his eyes shut.

George Cragg was another who had never seen the Grey Lady, but he knew many who claimed to have done so. "She was quite a talking point in the village," he said, his eyes twinkling, "and most of the talking was done in the Greyhound!"

To the best of our knowledge, there was no connection between the Greyhound Public House and the apparition. Nor need there have been, for the inn probably has ghosts enough. Tom Sayers, the famous bare-fist pugilist is rumoured to have trained there, and in the 'bad old days', when it was held at a yearly rent of sixpence, it was a popular venue for cockfighting. The local inhabitants were obviously a bloodthirsty bunch, for according to an entry in *Mid Sussex Through the Ages:*

> At the Greyhound Inn, Keymer, there was once a sporting landlord named Mark Taylor, whose hobby was rat matches. A terrier dog and rats were put in a pit, and the time taken by the dog to kill the rats was competed against by the next dog and so on. Betting on the results was often heavy.

Across the road on the lawned area that contains the war memorial, there once stood a district school. But in 1877, when the larger school at Hassocks first opened its doors, its use was changed to that of Church Hall and Sunday School. Nearby, four, two roomed cottages had been erected to provide accommodation for the men who built Hassocks Railway Station. Later, the dwellings were converted into two, four-roomed cottages. Then, around 1935, these together with the old school were demolished when the existing Church Hall, dedicated by the Bishop of Lewes, and costing £2,300 to build and equip, was opened by Lady Chichester.

Keymer Church is one of the very few in England which is dedicated to St. Cosmos and St. Damian, a pair of Syrian brothers and medical men who reputedly performed miracles in the 3rd or 4th centuries, and suffered martyrdom as a result. When the church was founded is not known, but it was mentioned in the Domesday Book, and for most of the time from then until 1536, it was served by priests sent by the Priory of St. Pancras at Lewes. Since 1752, the priests have been presented by the Brasenose College, Oxford, the Arms of which can be seen in one of the windows of the north aisle. According to Horsfield in his *History of Sussex*, the original building was:

> An ancient structure, standing on an eminence north of the village. In the King's books, it is recorded as a Chapel attached to the church at Clayton. At the west end is a low tower with a shingle spire (shingle being an early form of tiling consisting of split oak). The chancel is circular, similar to the one at Worth, and is divided from the nave by a circular arch. The pulpit is carved with a recess at the back. In the windows are some small remains of stained glass, consisting of an Eagle and flowered ornaments.

Most of what is seen today is from 1866 onwards, when major rebuilding work commenced, although much of the earlier style of the place has been retained in the design. The tower is built on the site of the vault of the Wood family of Oldland Mill, and the inscribed tombstone is incorporated in the wall of the belfry. A description of the church written at the end of the 19th century, mentioned that eleven of the windows contained stained glass, and that two of these were inserted in 1865 by friends and parishioners of St. John's Common, as a mark of the esteem in which Archdeacon James Garbett was held by this portion of his flock. The Archdeacon was Rector of Keymer from 1835 to 1879, and for some of the time his parish bounded those of Cuckfield and

Lindfield, and included St. John's Common. Most of the so-called 'cathedral glass' in the windows inserted in the second half of the 19th century has since been replaced with clear glass, with heraldic work done by Charles Knight of Ditchling. He was also commissioned to design and make the memorial window to the late Rev. W. E. Davis-Winstone, a former Rector of the parish. The work of another local craftsman, Joseph Cribb, a member of the former Guild of St. Joseph and St. Dominic on Ditchling Common, can be seen in the List of the Rectors, the first named being 'Master Peter' in 1230AD. There is a peal of six bells in the tower, but there seems to have been only three until 1911, when a Mrs Kirkham added to the number as a memorial to her sister. Two old bells retained in the peal are dated 1791 and 1866, and it is recorded that a bell dated 1713, which had some ancient coins let into it, was kept in the tower as a memento of the past, although it was not used. The original Rectory was at Clayton, but in 1914, when it was realised that the main population growth in the district was taking place at Keymer, it was decided to move there. Accordingly, a house in the Crescent, just a few steps from the church, was purchased from none other than Mr E. D. Stafford, whose first home this was, north of the Downs. His daughter, the late Mrs Salisbury-Smith, wrote about the property from a child's point of view.

> I think it must have been about 1907 or 8 that we first moved out from Brighton to the old Church House at Keymer. What a fascinating house that was, for children at any rate, though I can imagine it had its drawbacks from a parent's point of view. I seem to remember that the basement was frequently flooded to some considerable depth. My heart comes into my mouth even now at the thought of how my sister and I used to climb out of the window of the tower, three storeys up – scramble up the slates and sit astride the ridge of the roof. What a view! The return journey was even more hair raising, but we had no qualms at the time. Needless to say, that was one escapade our parents never knew about.

Church of St. Cosmos and St. Damian

Uncle Mac and Oldlands

The old rectory is long gone, but from their roof top perch, the two girls would surely have seen into the garden of a neighbouring property which in later years was to be the home of Mr Derek McCulloch OBE, a broadcaster better known to the listeners of BBC's Children's Hour as Uncle Mac. His full name was Derek Ivor Breashur McCulloch, and during the First World War he enlisted at the age of 17 as a private soldier in the Public Schools Battalion and took part in the Battle of the Somme. Cut off from his company, and close to the enemy lines, he was shot at by some German stretcher-bearers, a bullet destroying his right eye.

> "I wasn't quite done for," he is quoted as saying, " and being fearfully angry, fired back and saw one of the Germans fall. Then I feigned death. Soon after they went away I received four shrapnel wounds – in the right and left shoulders, in the thigh and the leg. My collarbone, shoulder-blade, and two ribs were broken, and a bullet was lodged in my left lung. I managed somehow to crawl to our lines. And then I recovered consciousness – in Hampstead."

After numerous operations, McCulloch recovered, and upon returning to active service, transferred to the Royal Flying Corps in which he served until 1921.

In 1926, after a short period in the Colonial Office, he joined the staff of the British Broadcasting Corporation as a London announcer. It was discovered that he had a natural flair for this sort of work, which resulted in his becoming an organiser for the Children's Hour Programme in 1933, and the Children's Hour Director in 1938. The appointment coincided with a motoring accident which was to cost him dear, the loss of his left leg, many more operations and a lifetime of pain. When he next spoke to the microphone he was on crutches. However, the loss of physical mobility in no way affected his determination to provide the best broadcasting possible for his children. He became famous for making a noise like a sheep when playing Larry the Lamb in the Toytown series, probably the most loved Children's Hour Programme ever. Despite his own misfortunes, Uncle Mac was always ready to help deserving causes. One of his radio appeals made early in the Second World War, was for £1500 for a mobile X-ray unit. The response exceeded £11,000. Leaving the BBC in 1950, he became Children's Editor for the *News Chronicle* for three years. He was also a children's author, a freelance lecturer and broadcaster, as well as a regular contributor to the *Radio Times*, *The Listener* and *Daily Telegraph* etc.

Derek McCulloch died on 1st June 1967, and in an obituary published in *The Times* newspaper, it stated:

> His memorial rests in the hearts of an astonishing number of people in this country whose first affectionate memories of broadcasting spring from listening to Children's Hour, whether as children, parents or as grandparents.
>
> When the BBC finally dropped the programme in 1965, it was a sad blow for many, including McCulloch himself, who became so well known for his signing off words:
>
> "Goodnight children –everywhere."

Returning briefly to the young Miss Staffords and their roof-top escapades, they would also have had a fine view of the track that links Ockley Lane with Lodge Hill at Ditchling.

A short distance along that track, one passes a house of considerable antiquity called Oldlands. Indeed the entire area is known as Oldlands, and as "Oldlond" it is mentioned in the surrender by the Prior and Convent of Lewes of their lands to Henry VIII, after which Sir Richard Michelbourne (son-in-law of William Campion

Oldland Mill House and a view of the mill.

of Combwell) conveyed it to Thomas Turner, and with regard to the Turners, we assume they inhabited the property as tenants before this date, as it is recorded on a stained glass window in Keymer Church. that they lived there from 1540 to 1861. In addition there are mural tablets to their memory in both Ditchling and Keymer Churches between 1681 and 1880. More can be learnt about them, or at least a Mr Richard Turner, from examination of the diary kept by his nephew, Thomas Marchant of Little Park, a gentleman with whom we have already been acquainted.

Further up the lane is Oldland Mill House, and Oldland Mill itself, which is reputedly the oldest surviving post-mill in Sussex, being mentioned in the Ditchling Churchwarden's Accounts of 1755. The mill ceased to be operated as such early in the 20th century, and in 1927, the Turner family who owned both the Mill House and the mill, conveyed the latter to the Sussex Archaeological Society, but that body, while accepting the premises, undertook no financial obligation for its upkeep. The result of course was that the fabric of the building deteriorated, and it was not until a group of concerned individuals (whose number included the well known artist, Sir Frank Brangwyn) raised funds, that repairs were effected. After which it was used as a museum, and those who wished, upon purchasing an entrance ticket from the resident of the Mill House (Mrs Webster-Wedderburn) could examine a collection of ancient agricultural implements. Not really surprisingly, it was a commercial failure, costs exceeded income, and after a while the venture was abandoned, so once again the old mill was left to the mercy of the elements, and once again its condition deteriorated, this time to the point of virtual collapse. But then, yet another group, the 'Hassocks Amenity Association' came to the rescue. In what must have been in the very nick of time, they leased the structure from the Archaeological Society and commenced the long and expensive task of restoration. The job is not completed, but the fact that the mill still stands and its future seems assured, is entirely due to the hard work and dedication of these people.

The Mill House is an ancient premises and it is thought that a habitation has been on the site since Roman times. This is probably true, for in an article describing the property that appeared in the *Sussex County Magazine*, Viscountess Wolseley said:

> If we search the brickwork at the south-west end of the house we shall find some interesting old Roman tiles. They are low down in the foundation of the house and are rather long and narrow.

While on the subject of mills, it is worth noting that the Domesday Survey records that there were two in Keymer. Horsfield's *History of Sussex* states:

> One remains at the present day, the other, which stood near the source of the spring, issuing from the margins of the Downs, has disappeared many years.

The first we take to be the Oldland windmill, while the second, the one near to the Downs, was presumably a watermill. Horsfield also mentions a third, the watermill at Valebridge pond (he calls it Wallbridge) which at the time was within the rural parish of Keymer. He relates a story of the place which although well-known, is still worth re-telling:

> On Wallbridge Common, is a large pond, which extends the whole length of the common from east to west. The ancient mill house stood considerably below the pond bay, when some years ago, the pressure of water against it being very great, it was forced away, and the water rushed with an impetuous torrent through the house, carrying everything before it. Among the rest, a bed on which a woman, lay reposing was driven down the stream, but fortunately, was impeded in its progress by some branches of trees which were in the way, when she was rescued from her perilous situation without sustaining any injury.

Ditchling

Lodge Hill ~ The Pageant ~ Ditchling Court ~ Wings Place ~ The Church ~ W.H. Hudson ~ A Village Naturalist ~ The Great Fire ~ Two Coaching Men ~ Doctor and Nurse ~ Vine Cottage ~ The Bull Hotel ~ Epilogue

Head east along the bridle track from Oldlands, peep through the gaps of hedgerow and coppice, and there are distant glimpses of delightful countryside all around. And upon reaching the summit of Lodge Hill, that curious mound standing just west of the village of Ditchling, some of the most beautiful views in Sussex open out before you. From here can be seen the rounded form of Wolstonbury Hill, the Clayton windmills, the imposing outline of Ditchling Beacon and the tree-clad crown of Blackcap, while to the west is the level land towards Cowfold, and to the north, the forest heights of Ardingly. Glance down, and seemingly at your feet is the village itself, church, pond, farmhouse, school (now a museum) and village green (once the farmyard). It is an idyllic, timeless tableau, an enchanting view of old England, and a memory to cherish.

The Pageant

Ditchling has considerable history, and in Lodge Hill it has a natural stage, so when in 1950 it was decided to perform a historical pageant, it was here that it was performed. Mrs Margaret Greenwood, a lady with previous experience on the professional stage, and who had produced many plays for the village theatrical society, was the Pageant-mistress, while the local vicar the Reverend Arthur Chichester Crookshank, was the author.

It opened at the time of King Alfred in the ninth century. Whether it was here that the monarch let the cakes burn is doubtful, but it is known that Ditchling was one of his royal manors, and that he did pay a visit to it in the year 898AD. So the first episode of the pageant commenced with a discussion among the villagers as to how best welcome their liege-lord.

But before this came the prologue, spoken by St. Margaret of Antioch (played by the late Tessa Donovan) about whom one correspondent wrote:

> This was one of the most entrancing features of the show. I never before heard of this saint, but if she were as lovely as the lady who represents her, and if all her movements combined such exquisite grace with dignified holiness, and if she spoke with so winning and musical a voice – I should very much like to have known her.

The writer must have been truly delighted, as St. Margaret spoke before each episode, explained to the audience what was to come next, and then returned to her seat in the background.

Tessa Donovan as St. Margaret

Rehearsing on Lodge Hill. Margaret Greenwood is to the left of the picture and the gentleman with raised hand is Reverend Crookshank.

In this manner, the history of the village was revealed through the passing centuries. The building of the church: the granting of a royal charter for the Ditchling Fair: a clash between Cavaliers and Roundheads, a pamphleteering conflict between the vicars of Ditchling and Westmeston, and a dance round the Maypole. In the final act, the performers grouped round St. Margaret and sang the chorale composed for the occasion by Mr John Greenwood, the husband of the producer. The pageant ended with an old grey horse (described in an article in *The Times* newspaper, "as a necessity on such occasions") taking its bow with the rest of the cast, as the spectators clapped their appreciation and thanks.

The dance around the Maypole showing the view from Lodge Hill.

Ditchling Fair, 1950 – Procession passing Freddie Green's sweet shop in the Lewes Road, Pat Gwynne holding the reins and accompanied by Peggy Woolley

Ditchling Court

At the foot of Lodge Hill stands a handsome white dwelling called Ditchling Court, and many years ago when farmer John Brown was in residence, its land extended as far as Patcham. In those days, hunting was a passion shared by the vast majority of country folk whether rich or poor, and the house was a popular meeting spot for many packs, including the Surrey staghounds. They were very large meets indeed, and the occasions were treated as unofficial public holidays. In his book, *Round about a Sussex Village*, the author, Fred F. Wood, describes the way it used to be:

> At one meet I recollect seeing, as a boy, what must have been over two hundred horsemen, and no end of traps and pedestrians, and three four-in-hands. Then the deer used to be uncarted just over the railway bridge on the Common. The deer-cart went up first, then the field and traffic, and lastly the hounds which were kept back until the deer had sufficient 'law' or start. On this occasion, there was a procession from the village to the Common.

Ditchling Court, the pond and Lodge Hill

View of Ditchling Common – north of the railway line

Wings Place

Standing close to the village green is Wings Place, an old Tudor dwelling that architecturally and historically speaking is surely the gem in Ditchling's crown. Clayton windmills apart, it must be the most familiar building in Mid Sussex, and in all probability is also (with varying degrees of accuracy) the most written about. That it is exceedingly ancient there is no question, but the early history is far from clear. There are legends of course, they are difficult to avoid with a property such as this, but what we know as fact is that it was the birthplace of Doris Hall, the historian and a writer on local matters. That lady, when describing her childhood in *Growing up in Ditchling*, tells us that the house was divided into four tenements. her family living in the westernmost. She said that the outside staircase was added as late as the 19th century, at a time when the room to which it led was used as a library run by a Mrs Turner. Apparently it was constructed simply to prevent those who used the facility from passing through the house.

In 1894, Wings Place was put up for auction, and the vendors, in an attempt to stimulate public awareness, blatantly blended fact and fable in a notice advertising the forthcoming sale:

Wings Place

> Lot 3, West Street. In the village of Ditchling, Sussex, an Ancient Mansion of great Historical and Antiquarian interest known as 'Wings Place', said to have been built by King Alfred the Great, and believed to have been described in the Domesday Book, but the vendors do not guarantee the accuracy of these statements.

It is as well that no guarantees were made, for with regards to this notice, Henry Cheal, author of *The History of Ditchling* (still the best book ever written about the village) had this to say:

> "Much as we revere the ancient mansion, and would even claim for its age four or five centuries, we regret we cannot find any evidence to lead us to the conclusion that it dates back to the time of King Alfred."

Mr Cheal added,

> "This legend, however, is only one of many connected with the place, and is almost as good as the one we heard a short while since, when we enquired of an inhabitant the origins of the name, 'Wings Place', and were told that it was originally Winn's, so named from a Miss Winn, who lived there in the days of William the Conqueror, and moreover, that the monarch used to visit her there, and subsequently married her!"

The Church

Standing on an elevated piece of land adjacent to the village green is the parish church. It is dedicated to St. Margaret, a lady who (mentioned in the Pageant) suffered martyrdom at Antioch in the third century. The building, which is very pleasant to look upon, has been described as "one of the finest of the Sussex hillside churches, being just in its proportions and beautiful in its details." few would disagree with these sentiments. It is cruciform in plan and built of flints with stone dressings, while the roofing consists of tiles and Horsham stone. The blunt spire is covered with shingles and contains eight bells and a clock. These bells are inscribed as follows:

> No's 1, 3 and 4. "Lester and pack of London, fecit 1766."
>
> No 2. "Peace and Good neighbourhood." Lester and Pack of London, fecit.
>
> No.5. "Edwd. Harraden, Thos/ Field, and Jas. Wood, Churchwardens." Lester and Pack of London, 1766.
>
> No.6. "To the glory of God and to the memory of Thomas Hutchinson, Vicar, 1883". Cast by Gillett and Co., Croydon, 1884
>
> No's 7 and 8. "To the glory of God." Cast by Gillet and Co., Croydon, 1914.

Apparently the church was noted for the high quality and sweet sound of its choir, which perhaps explains the old couplet, "Ditchling Singers and Bolney Ringers." Regarding such musical matters, Mr Cheal related the following story:

> The Ditchling singers took an eventful journey to Henfield, or some other village out west, to sing at a festival. The journey was made in a cart. Returning home, a few took the cart, leaving the others to walk. Those in the cart made a long stay at the Shepherd and Dog at Fulking. Here the walking party arrived, and seeing the cart outside, took possession and drove on. The party at the inn looked upon this as a trick, and with all possible speed took a short cut across country and caught them up. Then took place a fierce fight for the possession of the cart, which was a sad ending indeed for the Sunday excursion. It is said that the then Vicar of Ditchling did not venture to reproach his choir individually for their conduct, but preached a sermon the following Sunday on the text, "See that ye fall not out by the way."

W. H. Hudson

The author, W. H. Hudson, stayed at Ditchling during the early part of the 20th century, and his book *Nature in Downland*, contains several fond reminiscences of his visit:

> The church possessed that which to my mind made it the most perfect sacred edifice in all the Downs district – namely a family of white owls, strictly protected by the parson, tamer than most birds of their kind. The nest, or breeding hole, was under the eaves, and after the young were hatched, every evening just when the sun went down behind the great round hills, strange noises would begin to issue from the hole; sounds as if of a sleeper with a bad cold in his head, uncomfortably breathing through his nose, prolonged, sibilant, and tremulous, and occasionally deeper as if in imitation of the death rattle in a human throat. These noises were uttered by the young birds crying for their tea, breakfast or whatever we like to call their first meal. And presently the old owls would shuffle out to fly about the village in their usual flopping, unballasted aimless manner, this way and that, seemingly at random, as if they had lost their steering intelligence. But in twenty minutes to half an hour one would be back from the neighbouring rickyard with a mouse in his claws.
>
> Seated on one of the lichen-stained tombstones, or in a chair on a small lawn abutting on the churchyard, each evening while waiting for the owls to come out, I found my sight resting with a rare and untiring pleasure on the church before me; so perfect a building it was of its kind, so well placed on its mound with the old red-tiled houses harmoniously grouped about it, and so noble a background had the picture in the great round darkening hills and the luminous evening sky – I forget who it was who said of some peaceful village churchyard, that it made one in love with death to be in such a place.

Ditchling Church

A Village Naturalist

Had they ever met, W. H. Hudson and Frederick F. Wood would have surely found they had much in common. Both men were acute observers of the world about them, both wrote about it in a most compelling manner, and while Wood did not possess Hudson's literary genius, his accurate and unsentimental compositions of past life in and around the village, make for fascinating reading. Mr Wood's own life and interests also make for fascinating reading, especially when recounted by yet another Ditchling author, Marcus Woodward, in an article published by the *Sussex County Magazine,* parts of which we reproduce here:

> It is as a field naturalist that I knew him (Wood) best, and I know few who have a more intimate knowledge of our Sussex wild life. To Ditchling he has been unswervingly devoted through life, and except for a few journeys to London and one sporting trip to the north, he has never travelled further abroad than a day's march from his home. His own countryside he knows, and loves, every field and stream.

Frederick F. Wood

> The study of birds has been his lifelong interest, and all he has learned, he has learned direct from nature. His records show that he has identified 108 species of birds about Ditchling, birds of the Weald and Downs, and he has found most of their nests. He usually keeps a few pet birds; a raven is contentedly at home with him, and there is a jackdaw which will follow his master through the village.

Marcus Woodward goes on to tell us that Fred Wood was a recognised authority on Sussex wild flowers, having identified 700 different plants. In addition he bred butterflies and moths, and had identified over 400 species of the latter in Ditchling alone. he also had a collection of 1500 beetles!

Mr Wood was a palaeontologist, a stamp collector and a collector of pewter, and his cottage, Eastons, at North End, was a virtual museum that housed his many interests. Sporting prints, old books, old china and glass, and old furniture were on display in every nook and cranny, while all kinds of oddments could be seen in his cabinets. These included a tiny parasol with a folding handle which came from Mr Gladstone's sister; a Bristol salt-cellar shaped like a jack-boot; an iron lion for a mantle ornament; an ancient cheese knife like a sickle, with a razor sharp blade; old glasses for ripening grapes on a vine, and many, many more quaint relics.

Fred Wood's history is long and fascinating, indeed it is far too long for us to record here, so we will conclude with yet another aspect of this remarkable man, as told by Mr Woodward.

> I could write a volume of the stories I have heard him tell of his hunting adventures and his adventures among birds, of the deeds of derring-do performed by his packs or ratting terriers, of poaching exploits in youth and of his fights. He is a born fighting man; most nights he strips in his kitchen-gymnasium and, for lack of a sporting partner, punches the ball. Now and again a young boxer seeking reputation in the ring will find him out for a lesson – and go away sadder and wiser.

The Great Fire

Before 1919, there was no village hall at Ditchling, and public meetings were usually held at Chichester House in the High Street. Where the hall stands today, there used to be an attractive 18th century building called Eastfield House, which since 1893 had been run as a boy's boarding school. During the early hours of April 12th, 1919, a time when the lads had all gone home for the Easter holidays, the only people resident at the premises were Mr Branfoot, the Headmaster, his sister, Miss Branfoot, the Matron, three servants, and Captain Wilson, a former pupil on visit to his old school. They had all retired for the night, when Captain Wilson, whose quarters were at the front of the house, awoke to discover that the property was on fire. Despite his room being engulfed in flames, he managed to raise the alarm, then climbed out of the window and lowered himself to the ground by means of the thick ivy that grew against the outside wall.

In fact everyone escaped, but not before the headmaster, who, realising that one of the kitchen maids was unaccounted for, pluckily re-entered the blazing building and after locating the terror-stricken girl, carried her to safety.

Ditching Fire Brigade were quickly on the scene, but all they had to fight the flames with, was one jet of water from a standpipe in Lewes Road, and initially the pressure from this was minimal. Realising that they were fighting a losing battle, SOS messages were sent to Hassocks, Hurstpierpoint and Burgess Hill. For reasons unexplained, Hurstpierpoint failed to receive the call, and therefore did not attend, but in due course the Hassocks Brigade arrived, and then Burgess Hill with their steam engine which drew water out of the village pond. The spectacle as reported by the *Mid Sussex Times* was:

> ...a weird and sad one. The roof of the main building had collapsed and flames were shooting up like a volcano. Flames were also leaping through the windows, licking the walls, and sending sparks and fiery darts into the darkness. But the firemen fought like heroes and saved the schoolroom and dining room.

In fact very little was saved at all. The building which had consisted of a fine entrance hall, drawing room, study kitchen, pantry and scullery, as well as eight bedrooms and two large dormitories, was gutted and quite beyond repair. The source of the blaze was believed to be an exposed beam that caught fire in a flue at the back of the kitchen chimney. That then was the end of Eastfield House, and in due course the land was sold and the village hall was erected on the site.

Two Coaching Men

By a strange coincidence, two well-known coaching men have resided at Ditchling. One of these was a Mr George Milsted, an amateur driver and the Director of a London Publishing House. During the 1930s, he was approached by the representatives of the Brighton Bus Company, who, in an advertising ploy, had decided to reintroduce a stagecoach service. Mr Milsted was offered the job of driving it for them, and accepted. The chosen route was a round trip which leaving Brighton on the London Road, crossed Clayton Hill and made the first change of horses at the Hassocks Hotel. From there it drove in view of the Downs via Ditchling to Lewes where the second and final change was made prior to the homeward run via Falmer to the coast.

In a letter to the *Hassocks and Keymer Talkabout,* a correspondent wrote:

> I remember him [Mr Milsted] wearing a covert coat and frequently he had a blue cornflower, the coachman's emblem, in his buttonhole. I was told that when the coach left Brighton, it used to stop in the Preston Road near the railway viaduct. The guard would then descend and extract a number of top hats from the boot. These were distributed amongst the male passengers so that they would be appropriately covered during the trip. I understand that seeing them trying on what to most would have been an unaccustomed form of headgear was something of a joke to passers-by.

The other coachman was Mr Richard Hunt, a most informed man in equine matters, and who was happy to pass on the benefit of his experience to those who cared to listen. They were many, and according to one who met him, it was a rare pleasure to hear "Uncle Dick" (as Mr Hunt was known to his coaching friends) spinning his yarns of the good old days on the road.

> The interest of my life [said he] has always centred on horses, whether those of the four-horsed coach proper, or the poor man's coach, the London 'bus' of the old

days. Their drivers were the descendants of the original four-horse men and were hand picked to suit the district they served. They copied their fathers' ways of holding their reins, carrying and using their whip and they also copied their dress – the generously cut coat, giving the arms play, the curly brimmed silk hat and the buttonhole.

> In my youth, I made an eight-mile journey daily on such a vehicle across London, and I travelled on every other route, always with an eye on the horses, absorbing every refinement of the art of driving. In a humble way the drivers were like captains of ships, and the passengers confided in them. When the motor came, the London General Omnibus Company owned some three thousand horses. Each driver had a stud of eleven, and they made long journeys. One old friend drove from Mitcham to Gracechurch Street three times daily, making a total of sixty miles in all. From the ranks of such men came some of our best four-in-hand coachmen, and wherever they be now, so long as there is an elbow to lift and a whip to raise, I will remember them with the coachman's greeting – "Cheer oh!"

Mr Hunt talked at length of his early days, and mentioned his first enterprise, the ownership of a livery stable in Hove, where he touched the trade at all points. This included the giving of riding and driving lessons, and supplying coach horses for doctors and fire brigades. Referring to those times, he said:

> At a horse show one day, I drove a very smart cob in a buggy having a black board bearing my name in gold letters. Lord George Neville was a steward, I have hunted with him with the West Kent Foxhounds of which he was the Master. I looked like being an easy winner when he called to me, "What are you doing here, Hunt?" "Showing this cob," I said. "I thought you were a gentleman," said he. "You had better drive out of the ring," –Perhaps it was a compliment.

Mr Hunt recalled incidents as diverse as runaway horses and runaway lovers. And he described a Brighton that we can only imagine. A town that contained horse-drawn traffic of every description: the private drag, the barouche, the victoria, the park phaeton and the ralli cart, with equestrians pulled up to form little groups of rank and fashion. He travelled in and drove many famous coaches: Colonel Somerset's "Hirondelle", running from Enfield, The Dorking "Perseverance" and the "Excelsior" from Tunbridge Wells. The "Item" from Brighton to Eastbourne, the "Defiance" running to Oxford, the "Vivid" running to Hampton Court and the "Old Times" to Virginia Water, and there were many more:

> In 1899, one of the best turned out coaches for many years ran between Brighton and London, the "Nimrod". The primrose body bore the names of the towns passed, "Nimrod" and his dog were on the door panels, and on the hind boot was the fox. In the next five years, the "Viking" was running between London and Brighton, and I often enjoyed what was to be the last genuine galloping stage between Friars Oak and Cuckfield.
>
> 1905 saw the last of the parcel mail running between London and Brighton, and one night I accompanied its coachman. Holding the team with three and a half tons behind them, coming down Clayton Hill at night was a bit of a novelty. 1913 saw me a resident at "Haresdean", opposite "the Plough" at Pyecombe. I then made the acquaintance of the "Venture" coach of Mr Alfred G. Vanderbilt. I must own to being somewhat prejudiced, as the fuss made about him was out of all proportion considering the many sporting gentlemen who had supported the road, year in and year out, unmentioned and unknown. Mr Vanderbilts's horses were American, they were not like our idea of a coach horse.

Mr Hunt's memory may possibly have been at fault here, for we understand that the "Viking" coach, like the "Venture", was also owned and often driven by Mr Vanderbilt. It too was drawn by

The Vanderbilt coach, either the "Venture" or the "Viking", changing horses at the Plough, Pyecombe

American horses, but was not put into service until 1908/9, which was eight, not five years after the date he mentioned. It appeared following the earlier success of the 'Venture' on the Friar's Oak/Cuckfield run to London, and usually covered the more westerly route too and from the city via Henfield and Horsham. It seems likely therefore that the 'galloping' to which Mr Hunt referred, took place when he was on board the 'Venture', which also suggests that his first acquaintance with that coach, and probably with Mr Vanderbilt himself, would have taken place much earlier than 1913.

But be that as it may, we do know that in the Autumn of the same year, Dick Hunt and his friend, Sid Truett, put on the 'Tantivy' as an afternoon coach from Brighton to Lewes and back, via Pyecombe, Ditchling, Westmeston, Plumpton and Offham, a beautiful route, but it could not last. The sport of coaching never recovered from the blow dealt by the First World War, indeed its doom had been sealed in 1896, when the Royal Automobile Club staged the first run from London to Brighton.

> On August 4th, 1914, I went to the gate of my house to see the 'Venture' change horses on its last stage down to Brighton – its last stage ever, as it was to prove. Mr Vanderbilt pointed out a placard posted on the hind boot by the military authorities in connection with commandeering horses for the Army. I jumped up with the object of learning the war news in Brighton. Mr Vanderbilt dropped his hand to the brown team, and the six mile stage was finished in thirty-five minutes.

Alas! Alas! where have they gone,
The coach and the bays and the greys?
Alas! Alas! where is it gone,
That light of other days?

Doctor and Nurse

Earlier in his memoir, Mr Hunt mentioned supplying horses to doctors. Dr Richards of Ditchling was a keen horseman, in fact he was probably more often seen in the saddle than on foot. For him, riding took precedence over everything else, and it was not unusual for a patient attending his surgery in Beacon Road, to be told that the doctor was out hunting.

He was ably supported in his 'healing' capacity by a lady named Nurse Binns, an assistant, who apparently not trusting any form of transport, chose to walk everywhere on her own two feet.

In the winter of 1919, when the snow lay thick on the ground, a family of gypsies were encamped in a Downland hollow above Wick Farm. One of the women was in an advanced stage of pregnancy, the birth was expected at any moment and Nurse Binns' help was sought. She made her way there, and fearing complications, sent in turn for Dr Richards. He arrived on his horse, the baby was safely delivered, and they prepared to return to the village.

Dr Richards, true gentleman that he was, would not hear of the nurse trudging back through the snow, and ignoring her protests, he with the aid of the gypsies (for she was rather large) lifted her up on the horse and began to lead it home.

The nurse was most unhappy with the arrangement and begged to be let down, then, as if in answer to her pleas, the horse stumbled and deposited the distraught woman into a deep drift of snow. She pleaded to remain there, preferring to freeze to death than to face remounting, but the doctor would have none of it. Calling for more help from the camp, he had her dug out and hoisted up again, and this time led her safely back to Ditchling. Poor Nurse Binns was never allowed to forget her tumble, she swore that she would never ride a horse again – and she never did.

Ditchling High Street – looking south

Vine Cottage

Readers may recall that Mr George Cragg, when describing Dale House at Hassocks, mentioned collecting blood for the grapevine from a slaughter house in Ditchling. That slaughter house is now a 'Friends Meeting House', and hardly surprisingly, little if anything remains to indicate its former use. Originally it was part and parcel of a butcher's shop at Vine Cottage on the corner of East End Lane and the High Street. The last butcher there was a Mr Andrews, and senior villagers will perhaps recall that before his occupancy, the business was run by the Jefferies family with Mr Guy Thornton acting as shop manager. There may even be some who remember the previous owner, a Mr Slater.

It was during Mr Andrews' time, that the slaughter house was sold to the Quakers, and a bungalow was built in the orchard adjacent to the cottage. Internal renovations were also carried out at Vine Cottage itself, and in the course of the work, a hitherto unknown and unsuspected cupboard was found in the wall. This proved to be an exciting and significant discovery, for the recess was not empty, but contained numerous legal documents apertaining to the history of the building.

The details dated back to before the turn of the 19th century and showed that from approximately 1730, John Terry, a wheelwright, lived at that address. He died in 1780, leaving his wife, Anne, as the beneficial owner of the property. It seems that she chose not to continue residing there, but let it to various tenants, one of whom was a Joseph Baker (also a wheelwright) who paid her an annual rent of five shillings. Anne Terry died in 1804, and in the following year, the aforesaid Joseph Baker, purchased the premises for £455 from the executor of John Terry's will.

The next change of ownership to interest us occurred in 1886, when Mrs Blanche Jessica Munster acquired the freehold. As a resident of Bloomfield (now Stafford House) it is unlikely that this lady, described in the deeds as 'Widow of Keymer' ever lived at Ditchling herself, but probably purchased the cottage as an investment. The Munster family were great property owners, and had interests in 'bricks and mortar' throughout the country.

The first real indication of Vine Cottage's association with the meat trade occurred in 1894, when Mr Slater, to whom we referred earlier raised a mortgage for £650 and bought the place from a Brighton dealer called Frank Coster, although for how long that gentleman had the possession is not clear. However, it is of interest to note that William Hammond of Lodge Farm, Keymer, granted the mortgage loan, and upon his (Hammond's) death in 1900, payments on the amount liable were made jointly to his descendants.

The most recent document in the bundle is a deed of conveyance dated 1927, which shows that a Mr Fred Jefferies, a farmer from Cowfold, purchased both the business and the premises for £1400. He traded in Ditchling for many years, and after his death, his widow continued to run the shop. She was a daunting individual and in most respects, a pillar of the community. If there was a chink in her armour, it was in following the hunt. Her old black Vauxhall car with its creaking leather upholstery, was regularly to be seen cruising in the rural district whenever the Southdown Foxhounds were in action. Customers took second place on such occasions. With regards to this, the author of *The Old Century,* who as a boy worked at the shop, described a time when he accompanied the proprietor on her rounds:

> The car was full of meat and poultry for delivery to her customers at Plumpton, and we went there via Ditchling Common. Everything was quiet enough until we were passing the City cottages, then she suddenly put her foot on the brake and cried out, "The Hunt! Look the Hunt!" She was not mistaken, for streaming round the corner from Spatham Lane came the Southdown Hunt in full cry, first the hounds, then the riders dressed in pink, and lastly the supporters on foot. As they passed, one of the horseman waved, Mrs Jefferies cheered, then the group swung south, galloped over the Common crossed the cattle bridge and vanished in a swirl of dust. It was a stirring sight and my employer obviously thought so too, for with business apparently forgotten, she reversed the car

Vine Cottage

and drove swiftly back by the way we had come. Noticing that the 'tail-enders' were straggling in a south/westerly direction across Mr Mugridge's fields, she continued to the village crossroads, turned right and caught up with the horsemen on the eastern outskirts of Keymer (near the little Pumping station). It appeared to be over for the riders were dismounting, nevertheless, she parked the car on the verge and, instructing me to stay put, climbed over the fence and joined the huntsmen in the field. I couldn't see what was going on, but there was a lot of noise and laughter, and upon her return about twenty minutes later, she looked and sounded like a younger woman. Chuckling over whatever had been said, and in a splendid humour, she drove me straight home, remarking that we had done enough for one day. Though whether that view would have been shared by the people of Plumpton is quite another matter.

The Bull Hotel

As our journey started at an inn, it is appropriate that it should end at one, and the old Bull Hotel situated close to the crossroads would seem to fit the bill. It has always been a centre of local activities, and never more so than when it was the headquarters of the Ditchling Quoits club. In the old days there was hardly a village in Mid Sussex without its quoits club, usually based at a local inn, and sides regularly visited each other for matches which were always hotly contested. There were no motor cars to make the journeys, so the players walked, cycled or, as was most usual, travelled together in a horse-drawn carriage or wagon, and amongst other places, paid visits to Albourne, Ansty, Bolney, Chailey and Haywards Heath.

There was what was described as "feverish activity" at the Bull Hotel when the club was getting ready for the season. The rink was at the rear, on the site of the present car park and consisted of four circular beds. Each was two feet deep, and filled with pure yellow clay which members collected and transported in wheelbarrows. The central iron pin would be driven about four feet into the ground to keep it firm, leaving a short piece protruding above the clay.

There were eight members in the team and they played in pairs, one pair from each side at each bed. The quoits varied in weight from ten pounds to fourteen pounds each and were pitched from a distance of twelve yards. As can be imagined, it was no child's game, and required a lot of skill and effort. The rinks were in use practically every evening and matches were held at regular intervals. People came from miles around to watch the games, for they were popular occasions, particularly when trophies were at stake. One of the regular Ditchling players came from Albourne – and walked all the way.

The Ditchling Quoit Club continued until the onset of the First World War, then it was wound up and the trophies and assets were distributed among the players.

Another annual attraction held at the Bull Hotel was known as the 'Ditchling Goose Supper'. According to an article in the *Mid Sussex Times*:

> ...it brings together jolly farmers, tradesmen and other residents, not only of Ditchling, but of Burgess Hill, Hurstpierpoint, Hassocks, and even as far away as Haywards Heath and Lindfield, and come what might – one evening a year must be set aside for this famous supper. It is the event which links the rush and turmoil of modern life with the free-and-easy "good old days", and surely all the time the Bull Hotel stands and there are geese waddling about our farmyards, so long will the supper continue. There is little formality. "Ditchling is a happy place," declared one of its residents, and then let out the secret that, "if I feel a little downhearted, I go and see Charlie (the landlord) and have a tonic".

There certainly seems to have been some magic charm about the convivial gatherings at the Bull Hotel – a supreme happiness and comradeship which was not always found at social gatherings in other districts. And it was not merely the rich flavour of the geese made even more palatable by vegetables and tasty apple puddings, but also the confident anticipation of a warm welcome and excellent company which year after year attracted to the Ditchling Goose Supper, people from a wide area. A further extract from the report in the *Mid Sussex Times* presents a nice picture of the proceedings.

> Mr L. Sharman proposed the toast of "The Town and Trade of Ditchling." They all knew, he said, that Ditchling was a rare old town, and they found a nice lot of old people there. He had been associated with Ditchling for many years, and he had never found a better little spot in Sussex, the trade and tradesmen there compared very favourably with those of other places. He coupled the toast with the name of Mr T. Lindfield (the local butcher) who was known far and wide, and they always saw his jovial face at these convivial gatherings (Applause).
>
> Mr H. Parkes then sang "Asleep in the Deep".
>
> Mr Lindfield, replying to the toast, said he had the pleasure of being in business there for forty years, and had always got on fairly well, and anyone might live in a much worse place than Ditchling. He tried to make friends with everyone, and he did not think he had ever made any bad friends. Ditchling was a nice little town, why should they not be happy there? (Applause).
>
> Songs were sung by Mr Sharman and Mr L. Harvey.
>
> Mr John Turner gave "The Health of the Visitors", which was heartily received. Something had been said that night about tonics for depression, but he thought one of the best tonics they could have – for it refreshed their minds and memories from year to year, was to see their friends responding so cheerfully to the invitations to their festivities (Applause). But we don't come to listen to windy speeches. We come for the geese, for the music, and for good company – we want nothing more.

Epilogue

Traffic congestion in Ditchling has long been a topic of discussion. How different it once was, is revealed in this atmospheric little vignette published in the *Mid Sussex Times* nearly one hundred years ago:

> The crossroads were unusually crowded at lunchtime. Men you could see who had left their work, women many hatless and some carrying babies, not to mention the children who ought to have been at school (for the bell had rung some time before) all gazing earnestly at the Downs. Being only human one did so too, but could see nothing out of the ordinary. the Jointure had the same quiet appearance as it had a short time previously, and the fields and Downs beyond seemed likewise. Being so bold to make enquiries, one was told to "listen" and listen one did. Faintly at first, then gradually swelling in volume, one heard the sound of a band; then round the bend in the road came the musicians. On they came, but their music had now given place to bugle and drum. Following behind were the soldiers of the 3rd battalion of the Royal Sussex Regiment marching four deep, all looking very hot and weary. Round the corner they marched, up West Street, and were soon hidden from view by the rising ground.
>
> With the passing of the column, the men returned to work, the women to their homes, and the children to school. The dust settled, the sun blazed down, the crossroads regained their normal empty appearance, and silence stole over the sleepy village.

Sources

Albourne Village Guide
A History of the Castles, Mansions and Manors of Western Sussex (Elwes)
A Sussex Farmer (William Wood)
County Weekly Magazine
Ditchling Dialogue
Growing up in Ditchling (Doris Hall)
Hassocks and Keymer Talkabout
Hassocks Guide Book, 1975/6
Highways and Byways of Sussex (E. V. Lucas)
Horsfield's History of Sussex
Hurstpierpoint Police Station Day Book, 1906/1910
Hurstpierpoint Village Voice
Memories of Hurst (Vivienne Manchester)
Memorials of Old Sussex
Mid Sussex through the Ages (A. H. Gregory)
Mid Sussex Times
Nature in Downland (W. H. Hudson)
Nooks and Corners of Old Sussex (Rev. P. de Putron, MA)
Round About a Sussex Village (Fred F. Wood)
South Eastern Survey (Richard Wyndam)
Sussex Archaeological Collections, Vol X1
The Brighton Garrison (R. C. Grant)
The Diaries of Thomas Marchant
The History of Ditchling (Henry Cheal)
The Irish Cyclist Magazine
The Old Century (Mark Dudeney)
The Sussex County Magazine
The Sussex Weekly Advertiser
The Times
The Worthies of Sussex (Mark Anthony Lower)
Through a Glass Darkly – The Life of Patrick Hamilton (Nigel Jones)
Village Memories (published by Hurstpierpoint Women's Institute)
Windmills of Sussex (Martin Brunnarius)

Also published by Mid-Sussex Books

Edwin Street and The Victoria Pleasure Gardens
Mark Dudeney and Eileen Hallett

From Pyecombe to Cuckfield
Mark Dudeney and Eileen Hallett

In preparation

The Pleasure Grounds of Sussex
Mark Dudeney and Eileen Hallett

The Old Century
Mark Dudeney